Survival Guide for Being Alone

by

Brian Terrell and Ron Koehler III

LONELINESS

NORTHWESTERN PUBLISHING HOUSE
Milwaukee, Wisconsin

Library of Congress Card 96-67891
Northwestern Publishing House
1250 N. 113th St., Milwaukee, WI 53226-3284
© 1996 by Northwestern Publishing House.
Published 1996
Printed in the United States of America
ISBN 0-8100-0611-1

Contents

CHAPTER 1

The Who, What, When, and Why of Loneliness

The who and the when of loneliness

Which of these people would we think are lonely?

- The elderly widow whose children have all died
- The wife and mother of eleven years
- The pretty 20-year-old university junior
- The 9-year-old boy who attends a Lutheran elementary school
- The 45-year-old successful business woman
- The recently divorced father of four children
- The popular high school senior
- The wife of a Lutheran pastor

What if we knew that all of them were Christians? Would we think that any of them could be lonely? Well, all of them are Christians, and all of them have expressed the same feeling, "I am so lonely." Yes, Christians feel lonely. Loneliness is a part of the human experience, and Christians are human. Christian counselors encounter many people like them.

Jesus, our Savior and Substitute, knew the most excruciating loneliness ever experienced on this earth as he cried out from the cross, "My God, My God, why have you forsaken me?" Forsaken by his heavenly Father; denied, betrayed, and abandoned by his friends; mocked, beaten, and crucified by his enemies; Jesus truly was alone—in the fullest sense of the word—as he hung on the cross.

Yes, Christians feel lonely.
Loneliness is part of the human experience,
and Christians are human.

Of course, the pain that Jesus experienced accomplished our forgiveness before God and has much more significance than just an application to our loneliness. But at times, we can identify with Jesus because we may feel forsaken by God. Our families may forsake us; our friends may abandon us; our enemies may mock us; but, in truth, we are not forsaken by God. He has promised us, "Never will I leave you; never will I forsake you" (Hebrews 13:5). We will discuss this sense of spiritual loneliness in a later chapter.

For now we need to know that Christians of all ages can be and are lonely. We have already experienced those feelings. Remember that time as a toddler when you suddenly realized mommy was nowhere to be found? You experienced loneliness. Remember that first day at a new school when you didn't know a soul there, and you fought back the tears? You were experiencing loneliness. How about the high school dance or party you wanted to go to so badly because "everybody" would be there, but you didn't have a date? That was loneliness. Remember those times of inner conflict you experienced at college, when there was no one who seemed to understand or even cared about what you felt? That too was loneliness. Then there was the time you made all those plans for a special evening for just the two of you, and your spouse never showed up and didn't even bother to call. You knew loneliness. You will experience feelings of loneliness again. Think about those days, weeks, months, and even years that follow the death of a spouse of 50 years. That's loneliness too. The feeling of loneliness can come at any time in our lives, whether we are young or old.

So, if someone is telling you, "You can't be lonely! You're married; you're too active to be alone; you're so successful; or you're a Christian," don't believe them. You or someone you love can be lonely. You or a loved one may be experiencing loneliness right now. Perhaps that is the reason for reading this book. Are you doomed to be lonely for the rest of your life? By the grace of God, the answer to that question is an emphatic "No!"

The what of loneliness

Wouldn't it be nice if loneliness was like the flu? We could just take some antibiotics, drink plenty of fluids, get some rest, and soon we would feel better. The problem is that loneliness is not a disease. It isn't something we "catch." Loneliness comes from within us. It has five aspects:

- an emotional (feelings) aspect,
- a cognitive (thoughts and perceptions) aspect,
- a behavioral (words and actions) aspect,
- a social (relationships and self-concept) aspect,
- a spiritual (faith, child of God) aspect.

In other words, as a personal experience, loneliness can affect our entire being as Christians. Each of these aspects of loneliness will be addressed in later chapters.

Loneliness comes from within us.

In psychological literature, definitions of loneliness have been related to an innate human need for intimacy, people's perceptions of themselves and their relationships, and a lack of social reinforcement. As Christians we would add to that list our perceived relationship with God. These too will be discussed in later chapters.

What loneliness is and isn't

We read in Genesis 2:18, "The LORD God said, 'It is not good for the man to be alone.'" The Hebrew word translated as "to be alone" comes from the root that means to disjoin, divide, separate; and as a participle—solitary, alone (with a sense of being forsaken).[1] God created us as social beings with a need for interpersonal relationships. However, there are also times when a person just wants to be alone for a while. At such a time, that person is not experiencing loneliness. Rather, he or she is enjoying a moment of solitude, as did the Lord Jesus who often withdrew to lonely places to pray (Luke 5:16).

Clarke Moustakas, in his book *Loneliness and Love,* makes some nice distinctions between being alone, being lonely, and being in solitude.

- Being alone is an objective experience of not being with others. Therefore, aloneness is simply a state of being.
- Being lonely means "some compelling, essential aspect of life is suddenly challenged, threatened, altered, or denied. . . ."[2]
- Solitude, on the other hand, "is a return to one's own self when the world has grown cold and meaningless, when life has become filled with people and too much of a response to others."[3]

As Christians, we would add to this description of solitude, including the sense of a personal closeness with God through prayer and meditation in the Scriptures.

Moustakas did not use the term isolation, but let us consider it in contrast to solitude. Whereas solitude carries with it a sense of peaceful quiet and calm, isolation leaves one with a negative sense of abandonment, neglect, depression, and anxiety at being separated from and by those around us. In later chapters, we will expand on these four terms: aloneness, loneliness, solitude, and isolation.

The why of loneliness

As Christians we know that the primary cause of the negatives of life is Adam's and Eve's fall into sin. With sin came a separation from God. With sin came a loss of perfect love for one another and for God. With sin came a loss of the image of God, replaced by a sinful nature that merits our temporal and eternal destruction. With sin came the experience of loneliness.

Loneliness is not a disease,
and it does not need to be a permanent condition.

Psychologically speaking, there are two basic antecedents to loneliness. The first is labeled by Peplau and Perlman as "precipitating events" that include changes in one's actual social relations and/or changes in one's social needs. Such events might include a death, a divorce or break-up of a relationship, or absence from home. The second antecedent is "predisposing and maintaining factors" that include personal characteristics and cultural or situational factors. For example, loneliness has been linked to depression, anxiety, a lack of social skills, and low self-esteem.[4]

Summary

Loneliness is an unpleasant, negative, subjective, human experience that comes from within us. It can be the result of actual deficiencies in our social relationships, or it can come from our unhealthy perceptions of ourselves and our relationships with others and God. It is to be distinguished from aloneness and solitude. Loneliness is not a disease, and it does not need to be a permanent condition. In view of God's mercy and by his grace and power, we will seek to gain an understanding of loneliness, to grow in our ability to cope with it, and to work through it.

In the following chapters, we are going to consider the experience of loneliness among Christians. We will turn to the Bible for our examples, guidance, and answers. We will use the understanding and techniques of psychology, as supported by Scripture, for additional information in dealing with loneliness.

NOTES

[1]S. Tregelles, *Gesenius' Hebrew and Chaldee Lexicon*, (Grand Rapids, MI: Eerdmans, 1967), p. 113.

[2]Clarke E. Moustakas, *Loneliness and Love*, (Englewood Cliffs, NJ: Prentice-Hall, 1972), p. 21.

[3]Moustakas, p. 40.

[4]Letitia A. Peplau and Daniel Perlman, "Perspectives on Loneliness," in *Loneliness: A Source Book of Current Theory, Research and Therapy*, edited by Letitia A. Peplau and Daniel Perlman, (New York: John Wiley & Sons, 1982), pp. 1-20.

Chapter 2

God Is with Us

God will not forsake us

Yes, it is possible for a Christian, a child of God, to experience loneliness. Loneliness can begin as a small problem, perhaps just a feeling that certain people don't care for us or love us. When we become convinced that no one cares for us, our feelings of abandonment can grow into a much bigger problem. In some cases, we might even think that no one would care if we would cease to exist. Even a Christian can get to the point where he or she feels that even God doesn't care! Anywhere along the entire continuum of loneliness—from feeling a little lonely to complete despair—we can forget or ignore the One who always loves us and cares about us. We may be so lonely that we begin to doubt God. We ask ourselves questions like: "Is God there for me anymore?" "Does he even care about me?" "You say God is there, but how can I be sure?" Behind all the questions lies one underlying feeling: "If God really loved me, I wouldn't feel this way."

Anywhere along the entire continuum of loneliness—
from feeling a little lonely to complete despair—
we can forget or ignore the One
who always loves us and cares about us.

While we sometimes can feel that way, nothing could be farther from the truth! When we were baptized, we became a part of God's family. It's very interesting that, as we look through Scripture, God anticipated that his own people would sometimes feel deserted and lonely. But God always comforts his family. God inspired the Scriptures to comfort us in all our trials. The prophet Isaiah expressed how God's people felt deserted at times: "The LORD has forsaken me, the LORD has forgotten me" (Isaiah 49:14). But Isaiah also recorded God's response to such thoughts, "Can a mother forget the baby at her breast and have no compassion on the child she has borne? Though she may forget, I will not forget you! See, I have engraved you on the palms of my hands" (Isaiah 49:15,16). David found the same comfort. He wrote in Psalm 27:10, "Though my father and mother forsake me, the LORD will receive me."

The relationship between a parent and child is one of the most stable. But in this world, even that relationship may fail. God reminds us that he will remain with us even when the close relationship of parent and child deteriorates and leaves us lonely. These passages aren't the only ones we can turn to for comfort. We can find similar passages throughout the Scriptures. We belong to God's family by grace through faith in Jesus. We can be assured and relieved knowing that God will also remain near us—watching, directing, caring.

Jesus ministered to the lonely and outcast.

Who were the lonely people of Jesus' day? Social outcasts in any society, the ones who have been pushed away from society, would seem to be those most lonely. Being alone, if self-imposed, can be pleasant and relaxing, but having it imposed upon you can be a difficult thing to bear. The people of Jesus' day who had to bear such isolation were people like the tax collectors, prostitutes, and lepers. To have been pushed away from others because they didn't like the kind of person you were must have been quite unsettling. Yet, to whom do we find Jesus often reaching out with the comfort of forgiveness? Those very people! It's no surprise that we forget that sometimes; our loneliness and isolation make it difficult to concentrate on anything except our own problems.

In Matthew 9:11, the Pharisees asked Jesus' disciples, "Why does your teacher eat with tax collectors and 'sinners'?" The Pharisees didn't understand or remember that those lonely sinners needed God's forgiveness and God's love. We sometimes forget how much we need the forgiveness and love of Jesus and how accessible they are to us. We sometimes feel that others shut us out or push us away from them. Those are the times when we need to remember that we still have God's love and forgiveness. God loves his people. He embraces us to keep us close to him. As God's children, we should not forget that he is always there for us. He is never so far away that he doesn't care about us. God will certainly never leave us or forsake us.

To have been pushed away from others because they didn't like the kind of person you were must have been quite unsettling. Yet, to whom do we find Jesus often reaching out with the comfort of forgiveness?

You may be tempted to say, "That's fine, but it still doesn't clear up the lonely feelings I have concerning my friends, family, spouse, or whomever." Sometimes even God's promises seem like empty words, but that's a temptation that comes from our sinful nature. We sometimes think that we are the center of the universe and that nothing matters but what we think and what we feel. As long and we think that way, we might conclude that somehow our relationship with God is not as important as some of our other relationships. We might even think that he cannot help us with our loneliness. When we are tempted to think that way, then perhaps we have forgotten some of the things God has promised us.

Promises from God

Do you remember Psalm 23? The writer, King David, remembered that no matter what the circumstances, God was with him. He wrote, "Even though I walk through the valley of the shadow of death, I will fear no evil, for [God is] with me" (Psalm 23:4). When we forget that God is there for us and is ready to help us, we need to be reminded of Jesus' own words from Matthew 11:28-30, "Come to me, all you who are weary and burdened, and I will give you rest. Take my yoke upon you and learn from me, for I am gentle and humble in heart, and you will find rest for your souls." When we lug around the emotional baggage that wears us down, we don't ever have to feel that we must carry it alone. God himself is there not only to help us carry it, he's there to help us sort it out as well.

God's people have felt lonely before

As we turn the pages of Scripture, we meet other children of God who experienced loneliness. The prophet Elijah comes to mind. He spoke to God about his feelings when he said, "I have been very zealous for the LORD God Almighty. The Israelites have rejected your covenant, broken down your altars, and put your prophets to death with the sword. I am the only one left, and now they are trying to kill me too" (1 Kings 19:10). Elijah actually repeated these same feelings to God in verse 14. When he repeated his thoughts, Elijah revealed to God how lonely he felt. He was so lonely that he really thought that he was the last believer alive. How comforting for Elijah to have God assure him that he was surely not alone and give him instructions on what to do from there! If only we would always remember to take our lonely feelings to God. We have the same privilege as Elijah. Our loving

Father, who has fulfilled his promise to save us, is also there to help us through our troubled times. He will help us with the answers and help us to continue on, just as he did for Elijah.

How lonely Peter must have felt when Jesus looked directly into his eyes after Peter had betrayed him (see Luke 22:61). Judas may have been the loneliest man on earth after his betrayal of Jesus (see Matthew 27:1-5). Judas, of course, is an example of one who did not look to God to help him with his problem. And what about Jesus? If ever a person felt loneliness, he felt it. When he asked his friends to stay with him while he prayed in the garden of Gethsemane, he found that he could not count on them in his hour of utmost need (see Matthew 26:36-46). One of his close friends, Judas, turned Jesus over to the authorities for a price (see Matthew 26:47-49). Another friend, Peter, denied that he ever knew Jesus when questioned about his relationship with him (see Matthew 26:69-75). Then Jesus experienced a loneliness that we, as Christians, will never experience. As he hung on the cross for us, he cried out, "My God, my God, why have you forsaken me?" (Matthew 27:46). Talk about being alone! Thank God that we will never experience such absolute loneliness. Jesus was forsaken so that we will never be forsaken.

Jesus understands our loneliness

The kind of loneliness that we experience doesn't begin to compare with what Jesus went through for us. But that doesn't mean that we will never have lonely feelings or even long periods of loneliness. And knowing that Jesus experienced such feelings doesn't make those feelings any less real for us. The question is how do we deal with them? Knowing that God is our loving Father certainly helps. It is also extremely comforting to know what the writer to the Hebrews tells us. He writes, "For we do not have a high priest who is unable to sympathize with our weaknesses, but we have one who has been tempted in every way, just as we are—yet was without sin" (Hebrews 4:15,16). Jesus knows from experience everything we endure.

*"For we do not have a high priest who is unable
to sympathize with our weaknesses,
but we have one who has been tempted in every way,
just as we are—yet was without sin" (Hebrews 4:15,16).*

To know that Jesus himself was lonely can open the door for us to talk to him about it. After all, if we want help with raising a child, we ask other parents what they have done. If we want to know beforehand what it's like to have surgery, we ask someone who has been through it. If we're apprehensive about stepping into marriage, we ask advice from someone who has crossed that bridge. It need not feel strange, then, to go to Jesus about feelings of loneliness. After all, he's been through it all and to a greater degree. The writer to the Hebrews went on to encourage Christians, "Let us then approach the throne of grace with confidence, so that we may receive mercy and find grace to help us in our time of need" (Hebrews 4:16). We can take our concerns to Jesus in prayer; he understands.

God always cares for his people

God has cared for his people throughout history. It's no surprise that he would record some of those instances in his Word so that we can see him in action, caring for those who are his children. If God did not want to help us with our problems, he would not have inspired a man by the name of Asaph to write, "And call upon me in the day of trouble; I will deliver you, and you will honor me" (Psalm 50:15).

It is also comforting for us to know that God does not have a prejudiced eye. We may often think that there is no one to go to with our feelings of loneliness and other problems. We feel that whomever we tell will never look at us the same way again. We may be left wondering, days, weeks, even years down the road: "Does he still remember the day I bared my soul to him?" We wonder, "Is he treating me differently because I let him look into my personal life?" We often set up roadblocks for ourselves because we worry that what we say will be brought up later or talked about with someone else. We think that many inconvenient situations may arise if we let someone else in on our problems. Because of our fears, we end up keeping everything to ourselves. The truth is, most of those things never occur the way we think they might. The most important truth is that God gives us no reason to worry about any of that. When we tell him, he understands and wants only to work things out for our benefit and eternal good.

God really can and will help us, and that includes during our lonely times. These words of David remind us of the special relationship we have with our loving God, "As a father has compassion on his children, so the LORD has compassion on those who fear him; for he knows how we are formed" (Psalm 103:13,14). God knows how we are formed and everything else about us. He even knows when we hurt. If there is one picture to hold onto from Scripture concerning how close God is to us, it is from another psalm written by Asaph. In Psalm 73:23 he writes, "Yet I am always with you; you hold me by my right hand." What better picture to hold in our minds than that of our gracious, loving, and caring God holding each of us by the hand like a loving father does for his child. If he holds our hands, we know that everything will be all right. Do not forget him. And do not forget that we are never really alone. He is there for us at all times.

God knows how we are formed and everything else about us.

He even knows when we hurt.

It is a truly wonderful blessing that God, our heavenly Father, has made us his children and has assured us that he is always present during every step we take through life. In his great love he has brought us into the family of believers. Just think about that. We are part of the family of God! As part of God's family, we are never really alone either. We have many brothers and sisters in faith. And every person in God's family is important both to him and to the rest of the family.

Paul explains it this way: "Consequently, you are no longer foreigners and aliens, but fellow citizens with God's people and members of God's household, built on the foundation of the apostles and prophets, with Christ Jesus himself as the chief cornerstone" (Ephesians 2:19,20). We have a special relationship with God and with his people. Therefore we are never really alone. Again through the pen of the apostle Paul, God assures us that each of us is important to him and to his entire family: "Just as each of us has one body with many members, and these members do not all have the same function, so in Christ we who are many form one body, and each member belongs to all the others" (Romans 12:4,5).

In the next two chapters, we will explore more closely how we may view ourselves as children of God and how loneliness can affect our view of our relationships with God and others.

Passages of Comfort
in Times of Loneliness

God is always there for us

God knew there would be times when we would need the assurance that he is there with us. It can give us some comfort to know that God is there with us no matter what we are going through. These are some of the passages he gives us to let us know that he really is there. (Italics are added for emphasis.)

- Exodus 33:14 The LORD replied [to Moses], *"My Presence will go with you,* and I will give you rest."
- Psalm 9:9,10 *The LORD is a refuge* for the oppressed, *a stronghold* in times of trouble. Those who know your name will trust in you, *for you, LORD, have never forsaken those who seek you.*
- Psalm 23:4 Even though I walk through the valley of the shadow of death, I will fear no evil, *for you are with me*; your rod and your staff, they comfort me.
- Psalm 48:14 For this God is our God for ever and ever; *he will be our guide even to the end.*
- Psalm 73:23,24,28 Yet I am always with you; *you hold me by my right hand. You guide me with your counsel,* and afterward you will take me into glory. But as for me, it is good to be near God. I have made the Sovereign Lord my refuge; I will tell of all your deeds.
- Psalm 103:13,14 As a father has compassion on his children, so the Lord has compassion on those who fear him; for *he knows*

how we are formed, he remembers that we are dust [that we are human—not divine and perfect].

- Hebrews 13:5 God has said, *"Never will I leave you; never will I forsake you."*
- Psalm 121:3 He will not let your foot slip—he who watches over you *will not slumber.*
- Psalm 91:4 He will cover you with his feathers, and *under his wings you will find refuge*; his faithfulness will be your shield and rampart.

God invites us to come to him

We sometimes need to be reassured that God is not just a spectator who looks in on our lives but does not interact with us. Fortunately he foresaw our concerns in this area. We can be sure that God is always there for us and is actively involved in our daily lives.

- Psalm 50:15 Call upon me in the day of trouble; *I will deliver you*, and you will honor me.
- Matthew 11:28 Come to me, all you who are weary and burdened, and *I will give you rest.*
- 1 Peter 5:7 Cast all your anxiety on him because *he cares for you.*
- Matthew 7:7 *Ask* and it *will be given* to you; *seek* and you *will find*; *knock* and the door *will be opened* to you.
- 1 John 5:14 This is the confidence we have in approaching God: that if we ask anything according to his will, *he hears us.*
- Psalm 42:8 By day *the* LORD *directs his love*, at night his song is with me—a prayer to the God of my life.
- Psalm 42:11 Why are you downcast, O my soul? Why so disturbed within me? *Put your hope in God*, for I will yet praise him, my Savior and my God.
- Romans 8:28 And we know that *in all things God works for the good* of those who love him.

We are not "alone" in our loneliness

We need never feel that we are so different or odd just because we feel lonely. Loneliness has been around for as long as man has existed. Scripture records many examples of how God's people were affected by loneliness or lonely situations. Yet God is there for us and he has given us the comfort of knowing that we have an automatic support group. We are part of the family of believers and, as such, we are never really alone. We may sometimes think we are, but Scripture reminds us that we belong to a large group—the family of God.

- Romans 12:4-5 Just as each of us has one body with many members, and these members do not all have the same function, *so in Christ we who are many form one body, and each member belongs to all the others.*
- Ephesians 2:19,20 Consequently, you are no longer foreigners and aliens, but *fellow citizens with God's people and members of God's household*, built on the foundation of the apostles and prophets, with Christ Jesus himself as the chief cornerstone.
- Galatians 6:10 Therefore, as we have opportunity, let us do good to all people, especially to those who belong to *the family of believers.*
- 1 Corinthians 12:27 Now you are the body of Christ, and each one of you is a part of it.
- Exodus 33:14 The LORD replied [to Moses], "*My Presence will go with you*, and I will give you rest.
- 1 Peter 2:9 But you are *a chosen people*, a royal priesthood, a holy nation, a people *belonging to God.*
- Deuteronomy 31:8 The LORD himself goes before you and will be with you; *he will never leave you nor forsake you*. Do not be afraid; do not be discouraged.

Prayers in Times of Loneliness

Dearest Lord Jesus,

I can't help it; I feel so alone. It seems like I've lost everything and everyone. At times I even think that maybe you aren't there either. Deep down I know that isn't true, but I can't help feeling that way. I know too that you experienced loneliness as your friends left you and you suffered on the cross. You handled it, Lord, but I feel like I can't. I need your strength and your support in this difficult time. I also need the assurance that you are here with me. I trust you, Jesus, to help me and to get rid of my doubts and fears. Amen.

Dear heavenly Father,

I'm feeling isolated. Even when others are around, I still feel like I'm alone. It's as if no one quite understands me and what I'm going through. I know that you can help. Help me remember that you are never far away. Time and time again you promised to be with me, even to the end of the age. I know that you are right by my side, but I sometimes forget. Stay close to me as you have promised. Help me trust your promises. I want your guidance and companionship so that I can overcome my lonely feelings and truly enjoy my life and the blessings you have given to me. Stay with me, Lord. Amen.

Dear Lord,

I know that you are always there for me, just as you promise in your Word. You are not the problem. When I look around, it seems like no one really loves me. I don't have many friends. I'm not close with anyone. I need someone to be close to me, someone to love. You see the whole picture of my life, but I can't see where you're taking me. I can only see today, and today I'm lonely. I was lonely yesterday, last week, and last month. Lord, I suspect that I'll feel that way tomorrow too. When will you answer my prayers? I'm not doubting your love or your care, Lord. You have made me a loving and caring person. It's just that I don't have anyone to share myself with now. Give me patience and a strong faith to trust in your judgment and your timetable. Lord, answer my prayers according to your will and give me the patience to accept your will for me. Amen.

Dear Lord and Savior,

I don't know what to do anymore; I feel so all alone; it makes me sick to my stomach. I don't feel like doing anything or seeing anyone. It seems as if nobody misses me anyway when I'm not around. I can't find anyone to talk to or to do anything with. I am miserably alone. I need help, Lord. I need the help that only you can give. You encouraged me to tell you how I'm feeling right now. I have sometimes forgotten to share my burden with you. I should have come to you long ago because you've promised that you will never leave me or forsake me. As your child, I know that you are watching over my life and walking beside me. I guess that I have forgotten that.

Help me remember to ask for your help. I know that you also promise to do what is best for me, Lord. I need and want people to like me and to care about me. Please help me out of these feelings of loneliness and despair. Give me confidence in you as my Savior who loves me and works out all things for my good. Help me find the courage to seek out friends, and when you provide them, help me be a good friend to them. I am trusting you, Lord Jesus. Amen.

CHAPTER 3:

The Child of God

In the last chapter, we were reminded of our loving God who has promised never to leave us nor forsake us (Hebrews 13:5). Nevertheless, there are times when we feel, and perhaps even believe, that God has turned his back on us and forgotten us. In order to understand this discrepancy between our perception and reality, we first need to understand ourselves better. In this chapter we will learn more about ourselves as forgiven sinful children of God. First of all, we need to understand the distinction between who we are and what we are.

Who we are

Who we are is our self-identity. In Galatians 3:26-29 we read, "You are all sons of God through faith in Christ Jesus, for all of you who were baptized into Christ have clothed yourselves with Christ. There is neither Jew nor Greek, slave nor free, male nor female, for you are all one in Christ Jesus. If you belong to Christ, then you are Abraham's seed, and heirs according to the promise."

This passage identifies *who* we are. We are all sons of God. That we are identified as "sons" is important. In biblical days, only the sons of the family received the inheritance because the daughters would marry into the inheritance of their husbands' families. Through baptism each one of us was reborn and recreated by the Holy Spirit as a "son" of God and an heir of eternal life in heaven. Notice that this is not a status that is dependent on gender. Sons here means "male" and "female" as well as "Jew" and "Greek." Paul's point is that we are special children of God and heirs of his eternal inheritance. Our being children of God transcends our ethnicity (Jew nor Greek), our socio-economic status (slave nor free), and our gender (male nor female). In other words, our being children of God transcends our earthly existence. It is the very core of *who* we are in Jesus Christ.

How does our self-identity as children of God relate to loneliness? Because our relationship with God transcends everything earthly, it also transcends our earthly relationships. This is what Jesus had in mind in Mark 3:31-35, "Then Jesus' mother and brothers arrived. Standing outside, they sent someone in to call him. A crowd was sitting around him, and they told him, 'Your mother and brothers are outside looking for you.' 'Who are my mother and my brothers?' he asked. Then he looked at those seated in a circle around him and said, 'Here are my mother and my brothers! Whoever does God's will is my brother and sister and mother.'" The earthly family of Jesus included Mary and probably her other sons born after the birth of Jesus. His true family, however, includes all the children of God.

Our being children of God transcends our earthly existence. It is the very core of who *we are in Jesus Christ.*

In view of this, when we are focused on being children of God, we can be alone—without any earthly relationship—and not be lonely. As children of God, our heavenly Father is always with us, and the Spirit of Christ dwells within us. During those times in our lives when we are without a close relationship with another person, we can turn our sense of social isolation into a sense of spiritual solitude by focusing on our relationship with God in Christ Jesus. We can be confident that he will make all things work together for our good—including this time of aloneness.

What we are

As children of God living in this world, we move about through numerous roles in our daily life. Strictly speaking, a "role" refers to the expectations assigned to someone in a given social position. The various roles we fill in our daily lives answer *what* we are. For instance, one of our roles may be that of fathers or mothers. There are certain social and Scriptural expectations which define that role for us. So *what* are we? Parents! As parents we provide food, clothing, and shelter for our children. We train them in the instruction of the Lord, serve as models of Christian living for them, nurture them, and give them respect.

Who *we are is not the same as* what *we are.*

In a given day, we may move in and out of several roles (for example, mother/father, wife/husband, housekeeper/grounds-keeper, employee, friend, neighbor, church member). In all these different roles, however, we are always children of God who do "parenting," "spousing," "friending," and so on. Our self-identity is not meant to be tied to any one or all of these roles. Our self-identity is centered in our relationship with God as his child. *Who* we are is not the same as *what* we are.

In a given day, we may move in and out of several roles. . . .
In all these different roles, however,
we are always children of God.

That distinction is an important one as we consider how we can overcome our feelings of loneliness and the depression that often accompanies it. If we overly identify with what we are (such as, being parents or being wage-earners) and then we lose that role, we lose our sense of purpose in life. Unfortunately, sometimes in our own minds, no other role can fill that void, and we slip into depression and emotional isolation. When we identify ourselves first as children of God, who move from one role to another, we are able to adjust to and accept the loss of a given role more easily. It will hurt, but the emotional pain will not be as pervasive or long-lasting.

Love and the child of God

As children of God, we are complex individuals. Our heavenly Father's expectations of us, however, are simple. In Mark 12:30,31 we read: "'Love the Lord your God with all your heart and with all your soul and with all your mind and with all your strength. . . . Love your neighbor as yourself.' There is no commandment greater than these." The Lord wants us to love him with every aspect of ourselves. That seems simple enough.

Our *self*, however, is quite a complex being. If we were to translate the above verses into psychological terms, we might say that God wants us to love him with all our emotional being ("heart" or feelings), all our spiritual being ("soul"), all our cognitive being ("mind" or thoughts), and all our physical being ("strength" or behavior). The fact that the Lord expects us as his children to love him in all these facets of our being implies that we have the capacity to control them all. But we cannot control any of these areas except by the power of the Holy Spirit whom God gives to us through the means of grace. Have we really thought about ourselves in that way? In Christ, we are in charge of what we think, feel, believe, and do in our daily lives because we are children of God and the Holy Spirit dwells in us (1 Corinthians 6:19)!

> *It's important to remember that we cannot love God*
> *unless he loves us first.*
> *And he does—unconditionally.*

As his children, the Lord has more to tell about us in the aforementioned verses. Not only are we to give him all our love from our entire being, we also are to love our neighbors (that is, everyone else in our lives) as ourselves. Psychologically speaking, this refers to our social being—our relationships and self-concept. We may wonder, if we have given all our love to the Lord, how there can be any love left for ourselves and others.

It's important to remember that we cannot love God unless he loves us first. And he does—unconditionally. He loves us perfectly and completely and fills us with his love through the gospel in Word and sacrament. As God fills us with his love, we are able to love him and to love others. Imagine that God's love is the vast ocean and you are just a shallow hole on the beach. God's love fills us like the water fills that hole. No matter how much water we take out of the hole in the sand, water will continue to seep into it. We cannot empty it unless the level of the ocean drops below the bottom of the hole. The only way that we can become dry and empty is to remove ourselves from the means of grace, the gospel in Word and sacrament. When that happens we cannot love God, nor can we properly love others. Jeremiah tells us in Lamentations 3:21-23, "Yet this I call to mind and therefore I have hope: Because of the LORD's great love we are not consumed, for his compassions never fail. They are new every morning; great is your faithfulness."

When [we remove ourselves from the means of grace,
the gospel in Word and sacrament]
we cannot love God, nor can we properly love others.

The love of God fills us so that we in turn can love him and others. Our love for him doesn't begin to match the volume of love God daily pours into our lives. Eventually, as we become more aware of God's love for us and in us, we are able to love as God wants us to love. Thus we are able to truly love ourselves and others.

For children of God, the essence of healthy self-esteem comes from God's gracious love for us that empowers us to have a God-pleasing love for ourselves and others.

For children of God, the essence of healthy self-esteem comes from God's gracious love for us that empowers us to have a God-pleasing love for ourselves and others. Feeling good about ourselves, because of God's love and forgiveness, allows us to feel good about others. We no longer have a need to put down others in our resentment. We no longer need to be dependent totally on others for our feelings, opinions, or sense of worth. In other words, we are better able to get along with others when they are around, and we are better able to get along by ourselves when they are not around. We will return to this thought later in this chapter. But now we need to learn more about ourselves as children of God.

"Self"-control

The following passages set the stage for an internal spiritual examination of ourselves in the light of Scripture:

- Galatians 5:16,17 So I say, live by the Spirit, and you will not gratify the desires of the sinful nature. For the sinful nature desires what is contrary to the Spirit, and the Spirit what is contrary to the sinful nature. They are in conflict with each other, so that you do not do what you want.
- Galatians 2:20 I have been crucified with Christ and I no longer live, but Christ lives in me. The life I live in the body, I live by faith in the Son of God, who loved me and gave himself for me.
- Romans 7:18-20 I know that nothing good lives in me, that is, in my sinful nature. For I have the desire to do what is good, but I cannot carry it out. For what I do is not the good I want to do; no, the evil I do not want to do—this I keep on doing. Now if I do what I do not want to do, it is no longer I who do it, but it is sin living in me that does it.
- Romans 8:5 Those who live according to the sinful nature have their minds set on what that nature desires, but those who live in

accordance with the Spirit have their minds set on what the Spirit desires.

- Romans 8:6-9 The mind of sinful man is death, but the mind controlled by the Spirit is life and peace; the sinful mind is hostile to God. It does not submit to God's law, nor can it do so. Those controlled by the sinful nature cannot please God. You, however, are controlled not by the sinful nature but by the Spirit, if the Spirit of God lives in you. And if anyone does not have the Spirit of Christ, he does not belong to Christ.

Every person is born with a sinful nature inherited from Adam and Eve. We might say it is a permanent resident—at least until the day we die. On the other hand, Christians also have the Holy Spirit dwelling within them. We might say the Holy Spirit is an uninvited guest. We did not ask God to come into our lives. In his grace, God came to us through his Word and made us his children in Christ through the Holy Spirit. For many of us, God first entered our hearts and lives in Baptism. From that moment on, a spiritual conflict continues to rage within each one of us as the permanent resident seeks to evict the uninvited guest, and the Holy Spirit battles with our sinful nature for control of our every thought, word, and action.

Every person is born with a sinful nature
inherited from Adam and Eve.
We might say it is a permanent resident.

The apostle Peter, in his first general epistle, tells us to be self-controlled and alert (1 Peter 5:8). When Christians speak of "self"-control, we actually are talking about "Christ"-control. Paul explains this in the previously mentioned passages. In Galatians 2:20 he tells us that when we live by faith, Christ actually lives in us. On the other hand, he shows us in Romans 7:18-20 that when we are sinning, it is actually sin, that is our sinful nature, living in us. In other words, we are not in control of ourselves. At any given moment in our lives, either the Holy Spirit in Christ or our sinful nature is in control of our thoughts, words, and actions.

Christians also have the Holy Spirit dwelling within them. We might say the Holy Spirit is an uninvited guest.

Therefore what we have as children of God is not really "self"-control. By nature we cannot choose to control our permanent guest, our inherited sinful nature. When God brings us to faith, he gives us the desire and power to love him and to obey him. Paul said it so clearly, "For it is God who works in you to will and to act according to his good purpose" (Philippians 2:13). When we become believers, we can "set [our] minds on" and choose to obey the desires of our sinful nature and sin ("sin"-control), or we can "have [our] minds set on what the Spirit desires" and choose to follow the lead of the Holy Spirit and obey ("Christ"-control).

Keep in mind that our choices are our responsibility. We are accountable to God for those choices. Therefore we cannot use "it was sin living in me" as an excuse for our sins—as if we have nothing at all to do with them. We are responsible for our behaviors. When Paul says, "It is no longer I myself who do it" (Romans 7:17), he suggests that believers can't say their sin is "just the way I am." By the grace and power of Christ through the Holy Spirit, we can change our mind-set; we can change our thoughts, feelings, and behaviors because God works within us.

It is also important to keep in mind that a goal of the sinful nature is to destroy us and our relationship with God as Christians. One of the most effective ploys Satan and our sinful nature use against us is the sense of spiritual and social loneliness. It comes in variations of the thought, "Nobody, not even God, cares about me anymore!" Slipping into depression, we slowly slip away from God.

Without the Spirit of Christ dwelling in us, we are controlled only by our sinful nature. As Paul says in Romans 8:6-9, the sinful mind does not and cannot obey God. However, by the power of the Holy Spirit and the love of Christ dwelling in us, we are able to obey God's Word and will. The power to obey is from God. The responsibility for obeying God is ours. We choose to listen to our sinful nature or to listen to the Holy Spirit.

As children of God, we have the power to love God and one another only because God fills us with his love in Christ.

What does it mean to obey God? It means that we love God, and we love one another. As the apostle John put it, "Everyone who believes that Jesus is the Christ is born of God, and everyone who loves the father loves his child as well. This is how we know that we love the children of God: by loving God and carrying out his commands. This is love for God: to obey his commands" (1 John 5:1-3). As children of God, we have the power to love God and one another only because God fills us with his love in Christ. "Dear friends, let us love one another, for love comes from God. . . . This is love: not that we loved God, but that he loved us and sent his Son as an atoning sacrifice for our sins. Dear friends, since God so loved us, we also ought to love one another. No one has ever seen God; but if we love one another, God lives in us and his love is made complete in us. . . . We love because he first loved us" (1 John 4:7-19).

Did you notice how our discussion of "self"-control led us back into our discussion of love and the child of God? The two cannot be separated. To have "self"-control is to have the Spirit of Christ dwelling in us. To have the Spirit of Christ dwelling in us is to love God and to love our neighbors as ourselves (Mark 12:31) as God has loved us. To love one's neighbor as oneself requires that we love ourselves in a healthy way as God has loved us. Such a healthy love relationship with God protects us from the feelings of loneliness that our sinful nature seeks to instill in us. One way God's love helps us overcome feelings of loneliness is by giving us a healthy sense of Christian self-esteem.

A healthy self-esteem

The preceding study of ourselves as children of God gives us the foundation for healthy Christian self-esteem. We can love ourselves because God loves us and dwells in us. However, there is more to it than that. A healthy self-esteem acknowledges both our obedience and our sin, our strengths and our weaknesses, our abilities and our inabilities. Two concepts will help us understand the idea of a healthy Christian self-esteem: self-worth and honest pride.

Self-worth. What is a realistic sense of self-worth? The Bible gives us an adequate profile of ourselves. In Romans 3:10-12 we read, "There is no one righteous, not even one; there is no one who understands, no one who seeks God. All have turned away, they have together become worthless; there is no one who does good, not even one." At the same time, we read in 1 Peter 1:18,19: "For you know that it was not with perishable things such as silver or gold that you were redeemed from the empty way of life handed down to you from your forefathers, but with the precious blood of Christ, a lamb without blemish or defect."

> A *healthy self-esteem acknowledges*
> *both our obedience and our sin,*
> *our strengths and our weaknesses,*
> *our abilities and our inabilities.*

Of our natural selves, we are worthless before God. The natural sinful mind cannot please God. In his love for us, God paid a tremendous price to redeem us from the curse of his law. He sacrificed the lifeblood of his own precious Son—worth more than all the gold and silver in the world—to make us his own. That saving action by our heavenly Father has set a new value on us. We are of great worth to God. Because God values us, we can have a valid sense of self-worth.

To believe only that we are sinners deserving God punishment (Romans 3:10-12) leaves us with a distorted view of our worthiness. As a result we think such things as, "How can anyone love me?" or "My life is so meaningless; I don't mean a thing to anyone!" These are some of the thoughts of a lonely person. However, because of Christ we know and believe that God loves us and cares about us. God invested more than gold and silver in us. He invested the precious blood of his innocent

Son (1 Peter 1:18,19). Under God's grace, we also realize that other children of God want to share their love with us, just as we desire to share our love with others. Finally, just as in Christ God has loved us, so we can love and feel good about ourselves.

Honest pride. Can we as children of God have pride in ourselves? The answer is yes, provided that it is an honest pride. In his grace and wisdom, God sets down guidelines for honest pride in Scripture. The following passages provide us with those guidelines:

- Galatians 6:3-5 If anyone thinks he is something when he is nothing, he deceives himself. Each one should test his own actions. Then he can take pride in himself, without comparing himself to somebody else, for each one should carry his own load.

- 2 Corinthians 10:12-18 We do not dare to classify or compare ourselves with some who commend themselves. When they measure themselves by themselves and compare themselves with themselves, they are not wise. We, however, will not boast beyond proper limits, but will confine our boasting to the field God has assigned to us. . . . But, "Let him who boasts boast in the Lord." For it is not the one who commends himself who is approved, but the one whom the Lord commends.

- 2 Corinthians 12:7-10 To keep me from becoming conceited because of these surpassingly great revelations, there was given me a thorn in my flesh, a messenger of Satan, to torment me. Three times I pleaded with the Lord to take it away from me. But he said to me, "My grace is sufficient for you, for my power is made perfect in weakness." Therefore I will boast all the more gladly about my weaknesses, so that Christ's power may rest on me. That is why, for Christ's sake, I delight in weaknesses, in insults, in hardships, in persecutions, in difficulties. For when I am weak, then I am strong.

- Romans 12:3-6 For by the grace given me I say to every one of you: Do not think of yourself more highly than you ought, but rather think of yourself with sober judgment, in accordance with the measure of faith God has given you. Just as each of us has one body with many members, and these members do not all have the same function, so in Christ we who are many form one body, and each member belongs to all the others. We have different gifts, according to the grace given us.

The Bible speaks of two types of pride. There is the sinful pride of conceit and a haughty spirit (Proverbs 16:18), and there is the honest pride of satisfaction and self-respect. Galatians 6:3-5 gives us examples of both types of pride. If we claim to be something we are not, we are fooling only ourselves. When we boast about our individual accomplishments and talents, we exclude God. Conceit is the attempt of people with low self-esteem to feel good about themselves. It doesn't work, because they are always having to prove themselves to others and to themselves. There is no real satisfaction or self-respect —only self-deceit.

> *When we boast about our individual accomplishments*
> *and talents, we exclude God.*

How does one achieve honest pride without crossing the line into conceit? It all boils down to the answer to this question: What is our standard of comparison by which we test our own actions? Galatians 6:3-5 tells us NOT to compare ourselves with others—what others can or cannot do; what we think others expect of us. Our sinful natures will use such comparisons to lead us into sinful criticism of ourselves and others. We may become resentful of what others can do that we cannot do, or cannot do as well as they can. Beaten down by self-criticism, we seek to put down others in a futile effort to build ourselves up in our own eyes. Such efforts are short-lived, and we soon return to the vicious cycle of criticism.

> *Our sense of pride comes from how God has loved us,*
> *has permitted us to use our abilities,*
> *and has blessed those efforts with success.*

The question still remains, however, If we are not to compare ourselves to others, then are we to use ourselves as our standard of comparison? This only proves to be another trap set by our sinful nature. In fact, Paul tells us in 2 Corinthians 10:12 that we are fools to compare ourselves to ourselves. If we set our standards too high and think more highly of ourselves than we ought, we will continually fail. This will lead to discouragement, depression and, eventually, despair. If we set our standards too low, we end up making excuses for ourselves and never reaching our God-given potential.

We can be honest with ourselves. We know that before God, we are weak, limited, and sinful creatures. But he loves us and declared us free of sin through Jesus. In addition he has given us our abilities and provided opportunities for us to use them. Our sense of pride comes from how God has loved us, has permitted us to use our abilities, and has blessed those efforts with success. God has made us a part of his body, the church. Romans 12:3-6 and 1 Corinthians 12:12-31 use the picture of a body. As parts of Christ's body, we all have different gifts, so any comparison between different "body parts" would be invalid. Also keep in mind, that God's gifts include both our abilities and our inabilities. If God has made us "feet" in the body of Christ, God has given us the abilities to do only "foot things." Therefore our inabilities to do "hand things" and "eye things" are also a part of God's gift to us as "feet." As God-created "feet," we belong to the body of Christ; we have a place in God's family; we have something to contribute for the benefit of others. That something is defined by our God-given gifts— our abilities and our inabilities.

Openly acknowledging our inabilities and weaknesses
to ourselves and to others reminds us how dependent
we are on the Lord and on the power of Christ
to make it through each day of our lives.

Thus, honest pride does not allow us to boast beyond the proper limits of the total gifts God has given us. We think of ourselves in sober judgment in accordance with the grace God has given us. This allows us to feel good both about our abilities and strengths, and about our inabilities and weaknesses. Openly acknowledging our inabilities and weaknesses to ourselves and to others reminds us how dependent we are on the

Lord and on the power of Christ to make it through each day of our lives. In this way, we give glory to God when we acknowledge the Lord for our abilities. We can say with honest pride, "By the grace of God, I did a good job on that project." We give glory to God also when we acknowledge our weaknesses. We can say with honest pride, "I didn't know how to do that and I have no talent to do it. Thank God you could help me."

Honest pride allows us to feel good about ourselves when we know that we have done the best we can with what God has given us. This is an important standard by which to test our own actions. It does not mean that we have to be functioning always at peak performance, but only at our best at a given moment. The circumstances God places in our lives on any given day influence our abilities and inabilities to perform on that day. God does not expect any more from us than what he gives us the ability to do. To think we can always perform at peak levels is to think more highly of ourselves than we ought. Such thinking will again result in discouragement, depression, and low self-esteem.

> *Honest pride allows us to feel good about ourselves when we know that we have done the best we can with what God has given us.*

So, how do we test our own actions in honest pride? Each day we take into account our God-given abilities and inabilities along with whatever circumstances God has added for the day. Our only goal is to *do the best we can with what God has given us for today*. Having done that, we give all thanks and praise to God, as we feel good about ourselves for another day. And when we make mistakes during the day and fall short of that goal, we comfort ourselves in knowing that we have a gracious and forgiving God who understands. The world won't end just because we made a mistake. We always look to improve and do better. And we learn from our mistakes; sometimes we learn better from them than from our successes.

A healthy self-esteem and loneliness are incompatible. Christian self-esteem is focused on our relationship with our gracious, forgiving, and understanding God. Our sense of well-being is not based on the standards of worthiness we set for ourselves or on those imposed by others. We can move about, within, or between our various roles with a healthy, God-pleasing outlook. The relationships created by those roles grow when we understand our relationship with God. In our identity as children of God, we are dependent only on our faithful God. We are not dependent upon the whims of others, nor upon the lies of our own sinful nature to support our sense of worth. God's love in Christ supplies a true and honest sense of self and self-esteem. God loves us just as we are. We are loved, and because he loves us, we love him and others. That leaves little room for a lingering sense of loneliness.

Summary

Who are we? We are children of God in Christ Jesus. In his grace God has given each of us a special set of gifts—our abilities and inabilities—which we are to use to his glory and to help one another in our various roles in life. In doing so we show our love for God, for one another, and for ourselves.

As children of God, we have both our sinful nature and the Spirit of Christ dwelling in us. They are in constant conflict to control our thoughts, feelings, behaviors, spiritual life, and social relationships. Through the gospel, God strengthens us so we can overcome our sinful nature. Then we can turn from the desires of our sinful nature to loving obedience to our heavenly Father and Savior. Only when God gives us the strength to overcome the power of sin that controls our thoughts, words, and actions, can we truly show our love for God.

As children of God, we realize that our worth as individuals is totally dependent on God's grace in Christ Jesus. In the love of Christ, we can acknowledge our weaknesses and our strengths and feel good about them both. In our strengths, we are serving the Lord; in our weaknesses, God's power is made perfect. Our sense of self-worth and self-esteem doesn't depend on the approval of others. It depends only on the gracious love and mercy of our heavenly Father who has made us his own in Christ.

If you are experiencing loneliness at this time, there is a good chance that your perspective of yourself does not agree with what has been set forth in this chapter. Chances are you may be listening to some of the lies that your sinful nature is telling you about yourself, your relationship with God, and your relationships with others. In order to check out those lies, you will need a better understanding of what loneliness is and how it affects you. This is covered in detail in chapter 4.

What Do We Know about Loneliness?

Psychological studies of loneliness

Thus far, we have focused on a Scriptural understanding of the Christian and loneliness. We began with a brief introduction to the concept of loneliness. Then we learned how our sinful nature can lead us astray into thinking that we might even be without God. We considered how our identity as a child of God can have an effect on our feeling or not feeling lonely, and that God gives us the strength to overcome our sinful nature through the gospel.

The authors of this book believe that we are better equipped to deal with something when we have a better understanding of it. At this time we turn to the psychological concepts of loneliness itself. In the light of God's Word, we look at what research in the field of psychology has taught us about loneliness. In the discussion of these concepts, we present information that will be helpful in dealing with loneliness. The reader should know that notes for this chapter and those following indicate the cited source of information. They do not necessarily cite the original research study.

At this time we turn to the psychological concepts of loneliness itself. . . . In the discussion of these concepts, we present information that will be helpful in dealing with loneliness.

Over the last 20 to 30 years, a considerable amount of study has been devoted to loneliness. Peplau and Perlman note that in all these studies there seems to be at least three points of agreement:

- Loneliness appears to be the result of deficiencies in an individual's social relationships.
- Loneliness appears to be a subjective experience, as opposed to the objective experience of being alone.
- Loneliness is an unpleasant experience that results in a state of emotional distress.

As Christians, we do not disagree with any of the above points. We do want to point out, however, that children of God have a relationship with God that transcends all our social relationships. God is faithful. He is always with us; he will never leave us. Even when there are deficiencies in our social relationships, our heavenly Father remains steadfast and true in his love for us. Nevertheless, our sinful nature desires that we perceive that God no longer cares for us and has abandoned us. Satan's goal is that we experience a state of emotional and spiritual distress, and thus begin to doubt God's place in our lives. (It might be well to review chapter 2.)

Approaches to the study of loneliness

Peplau and Perlman present three basic themes in the various approaches to the study of loneliness. The first approach is called the *Need for Intimacy*. From this perspective, loneliness is a response to the absence of a relationship with that special someone. This approach focuses on feelings, with the idea that no one can feel intimacy by him/herself. Intimacy is not to be equated with sexuality (see chapter 5). It implies a mutual sharing of our "self" with someone else. According to this approach, we can experience loneliness without even recognizing that we are lonely.

The second approach, the *Cognitive Processes*, states that the sense of loneliness comes from our perception and evaluation of our social relations. When we perceive a discrepancy between what we desire from a particular relationship and what is actually happening in that relationship, we become dissatisfied with it. This sense of dissatisfaction may be interpreted by us as loneliness because our social needs and desires are not being met.

The third theme in loneliness research is the *Insufficient Social Reinforcement* approach. This perspective begins with the premise that satisfying social relationships are rewarding to us. When we are in a satisfying relationship, we feel good, and we want to continue to feel good. When we are without such a relationship, or in one that is not satisfying to us, we feel deprived. Without the positive social reinforcements of a satisfying relationship, we feel deprived because our expectations have not been met. This sense of deprivation underlies our feelings of loneliness.[1]

As in most research findings, we see that there is some truth in each of these three approaches. No single approach gives us all the answers. Depending on how people view themselves and how they interact with the world around them, any one of the above themes may make more sense than the others. Nevertheless, each approach can provide some insight into the problem of loneliness.

The basic truth is that God created us as social creatures. . . .
Based on this truth . . . loneliness is a common experience
for all members of the human race.

There is, however, a basic truth that underlies all of the above approaches, even if the researchers do not acknowledge it. The basic truth is that God created us as social creatures. At creation he declared, "It is not good for the man to be alone. I will make a helper suitable for him" (Genesis 2:18). Based on this truth, we agree with the notion that loneliness is a common experience for all members of the human race. We all experience it at one time or another in our lives in varying degrees.

Changes that lead to loneliness

There are two types of changes that may lead to loneliness according to Peplau and Perlman:

- changes in our social relationships, and/or
- changes in our social needs and desires.

Changes in our *social relationships* might include a temporary separation from someone close to us, the death of a loved one or a dear friend, a divorce, the break-up of a close relationship, or someone moving away and out of our daily lives. The impact of these changes depends on the quality of these relationships and the personal value we have assigned to them.

Changes in our *social needs and desires* occur as we grow and mature and as we gain social experience. Throughout our lifetime we go through many personal developmental changes. Different ages have different needs and different social skills. In early childhood, we need our mothers the most, and we are not that concerned about forming any other relationships. In pre- and early adolescence, we are moving away from our relationships with our parents and are seeking stronger relations with our peers, first in groups and then individually. The social skills we used as toddlers may not work as well for us when we are interacting with our fellow teenagers. Deficits, either developmental or in the area of social skills, may result in our experiencing loneliness.

> *Because our personal social needs and desires*
> *are not being met in our relationships,*
> *we may experience loneliness.*

For instance, an intellectually gifted child is advanced two grades in school, placing this child in a group of more socially developed classmates with whom his or her age-appropriate social skills are no longer compatible. Until this child learns new social skills and develops social desires similar to the new classmates', the child may experience loneliness. In another instance, we may have developed socially beyond our peers and thus find that we lack significant and stimulating interactions with them. Because our personal social needs and desires are not being met in our relationships, we may experience loneliness.[2]

The apostle Paul serves as a good example of what Peplau and Perlman were describing. Paul traveled throughout the Mediterranean world on his missionary journeys. He knew that God's plan reserved sex as a blessing for marriage. He also knew that it was God's plan for husbands to live with their wives in love and consideration. It would appear that, because of his extensive travels as a missionary to the Gentiles and his tireless devotion of time to the preaching of the gospel, Paul knew that he would not be able to fulfill his responsibilities to a wife.

In his grace, God gave Paul the ability to go without a sexual relationship, so that his bachelorhood might be a blessing to him rather than a curse. However, this did not insulate Paul from feeling lonely. Paul still needed and desired social relationships and intimacy. He needed to have a sense of belonging, a sense that someone cared about him. This is most evident in his letter to the Philippians and in his second letter to Timothy.

> Philippians 4:14-16 Yet it was good of you to share in my troubles. Moreover, as you Philippians know, in the early days of your acquaintance with the gospel, when I set out from Macedonia, not one church shared with me in the matter of giving and receiving, except you only; for even when I was in Thessalonica, you sent me aid again and again when I was in need.

During Paul's first imprisonment in Rome, he was under house arrest. His friends were able to come and go freely. Yet it was important to him that the Philippians had remembered him. It appears that it was important to him to know that someone cared about him and his needs. He had a sense of belonging—a sense of community. He had a social support network that was adequate for his needs.

> 2 Timothy 1:15; 4:9,10 You know that everyone in the province of Asia has deserted me, including Phygelus and Hermogenes. . . . Do your best to come to me quickly, for Demas, because he loved this world, has deserted me and has gone to Thessalonica. Crescens has gone to Galatia, and Titus to Dalmatia.

This time Paul was in a dungeon. He knew he was about to be executed. His work for the gospel of Christ was drawing to a close. He was confident that the Lord would bring him safely into his heavenly kingdom. Nevertheless, Paul still longed for the companionship of his "true son in the faith"—Timothy (1 Timothy 1:2). Paul felt deserted and lonely. He had Luke, his long-time traveling companion and personal physician, with him. However, he had developed a truly close bond with Timothy. Knowing his days on this earth were numbered, Paul missed Timothy; he was lonely without him even when among friends. We might say that he was experiencing a deficit in both his social relationships and his social needs.

Antecedents of loneliness

Ami Rokach gives us another view of loneliness, involving three clusters of conditions that may lead to the experience of loneliness. She looks at those factors that may have contributed to the development of loneliness.

In her study, Rokach found that the most commonly reported antecedents to loneliness among her subjects were loss, an inadequate social support system, personal shortcomings (especially negative self-perception and social skills deficits), and crisis.

The first cluster is *Relational Deficits*, which includes "either missing relationships or present ones that do not fulfill the person's needs for belongingness, support, love, or intimacy."[3]
The factors in this cluster include:

- social alienation, such as separation from loved ones or isolation from others in general;
- inadequate social support system, such as a lack of those who care, a sense of not belonging, or a disappointing relationship;
- troubled relationships, such as disharmonious relationships that are unfulfilling or abusive and characterized by the absence of any intimacy.

The second cluster is *Traumatic Events*, which includes "significant and often dramatic changes in one's world, such as an important loss of a dear person or relationship, a personal crisis, or the uprooting and separation from one's family and familiar environment."[4]

The three factors that form this cluster include:

- mobility/change—moving away from one's familiar surroundings, friends, family, resulting in a sense of being uprooted and homesick;
- loss—bringing a permanent end to a close and intimate relationship through death, divorce, or breakup;
- crisis—creating a sudden, significant change in one's world, or a realization of one's limitations, uncertainties, mortality.

The final cluster presented by Rokach involves *Personal Character and Developmental Variables*, which includes "the more personal causes of loneliness . . . that prevent one from enjoying a good, close relationship."[5]

There are two factors in this final cluster:

- personal shortcomings—including fear of intimacy, negative self-image, and low self-esteem, a lack of social skills, a confining illness or disability, and negative experiences in past relationships;
- developmental deficits—including the lack of warmth, affection, security in childhood; rejection or neglect by parents in childhood; lack of parental involvement in childhood experiences; and traumatic experiences in childhood.

In her study, Rokach found that the most commonly reported antecedents to loneliness among her subjects were loss, an inadequate social support system, personal shortcomings (especially negative self-perception and social skills deficits), and crisis. If we were to review the previously stated themes and approaches to loneliness, we would see that every approach or model proposed to explain loneliness has something to offer for our understanding of the concept. However, no one model or approach has all the answers. Therefore, it is good for us to consider several views of loneliness, from which we can pick and choose what best fits our own experience.

Models of loneliness

Social and emotional isolation. Robert Weiss spoke of the nature of loneliness in terms of *social isolation* and *emotional isolation*. "The loneliness of emotional isolation is initiated by the absence of a close emotional attachment, and the loneliness of social isolation is initiated by the absence of socially integrative relationships."[6]

Weiss equated the sense of *emotional isolation* with the feelings of abandonment babies feel when they realize their mommy is gone. In other words, that special someone, who gives meaning and identity to life, is missing. There is a sense of utter aloneness even in the midst of a group of friends. Specifically, we experience emotional isolation when we lack a relationship that has intimacy. Intimacy is used here in the sense of a deep mutual sharing of self between two people and is not to be equated with a mere sexual relationship.

> *Intimacy is . . . a deep mutual sharing of self between two people and is not to be equated with a mere sexual relationship.*

In contrast, we experience *social isolation* when we are not participating in a social network of friends and family who share common interests with us. Social isolation might be equated with lacking a sense of belonging or a sense of community. When we are with others who share a common interest or experience, we feel like we "fit in." When this is missing in our lives, we tend to feel "left out."

Using Weiss' distinction of two types of isolation, we can see how we might be with many friends and still feel lonely because we do not have that special someone. We may have a sense of community but not a sense of intimacy. On the other hand, we may have that special someone, but no other person or group with whom to interact. We lack a sense of community. Then the two of us who share intimacy may experience a sense of social isolation. We have intimacy but lack a sense of community.

Aloneness, loneliness, and solitude. In his original research on loneliness, Clarke Moustakas made a distinction between being alone, being lonely, and being in solitude.

Aloneness refers to the objective reality of being without a companion. It can mean a physical state: "I am alone; there is no one else here." Or a psychological state can also be expressed: "I feel like I am the only one here." Neither of these statements necessarily implies either a positive or a negative experience. They simply say, "I am by myself—period."

Loneliness is always a negative experience. Moustakas saw loneliness as "the intense feeling of a breach of faith, a broken trust, the aftermath of a shattering realization. . . . In loneliness some compelling, essential aspect of life is suddenly challenged, threatened, altered, denied."[7] Loneliness is associated with the experiences of rejection, misunderstanding, not belonging, guilt, and emotional pain.

Concerning *Solitude* Moustakas wrote: "Solitude is a return to one's own self when the world has grown cold and meaningless, when life has become filled with people and too much of a response to others."[8] There are times in our lives when we just want to be alone. We go off by ourselves to enjoy the silence, the peace and tranquillity of being apart from the busy, noisy world of our daily existence. Solitude is a time for introspection and meditation.

As Christians we take the experience of solitude beyond that of introspection and meditation. It is a time for prayer, personal devotion, and Bible study. Such time alone allows us to reach out to God in prayer and gives God the opportunity to reach out to us through contact with the gospel. As we review our situation, we can consider the hand of God in our daily life. We can quietly review ourselves in the light of eternity and God's love as we contemplate our purpose in life as children of God. Being alone is not loneliness, but a time just to "get away from it all" and relax. Jesus often took advantage of solitude to be refreshed in prayer and communication with his heavenly Father. (Luke 5:15,16) As the news about him spread so that larger crowds of people came to hear him and to be healed of their sicknesses, Jesus often withdrew to lonely places and prayed.

Four types of lonely people. One research study (De Jong-Gierveld and Raadschelders) suggested four types of lonely people:

- nonlonely
- the periodically and temporarily lonely
- the hopeless lonely
- the resigned, hopelessly lonely[9]

The *nonlonely* appear to have at least one intimate relationship and a variety of friendships. They are socially active and belong to numerous organizations. When they are alone, they tend to enjoy it or, at least, do not mind it.

The *periodically and temporarily lonely* lack an intimate relationship with that special someone. However, they have numerous friendships, are socially active, and see their loneliness as temporary.

The *hopeless lonely* are those who lack intimacy in a relationship in which they expected to find it. They are very dissatisfied with this relationship and feel deprived of friendship. They blame others for their loneliness and feel hopeless about the future.

On the other hand, the *resigned, hopelessly lonely* lack an intimate relationship and also have few friends, but they do not express dissatisfaction, nor do they blame others. They tend to be resigned to their loneliness as a fact of life.

Time and loneliness. Our final model of loneliness (Jeffery Young) makes distinctions based on the amount of time over which a person experiences loneliness. The classifications are *chronic, transient*, and *situational* loneliness. "Chronic loneliness refers to people who have not been satisfied with their relationships for a period of two or more consecutive years. Situational or transitional loneliness involves individuals who had satisfying relationships until they were confronted either with a specific crisis such as death or divorce, or with a predictable developmental change like leaving home for college. . . . Transient or everyday loneliness includes brief and occasional lonely moods."[10]

Young explained that situational loneliness can last for a substantial period of time, depending on the intensity of the loss or change. Usually, however, the person does come to an acceptance of the loss or change after a brief period of time and is able to renew or establish new relationships. If an individual does not appropriately adjust to this loss or change within two years, Young would then declare the loneliness to be chronic. In such cases, the chronically lonely person has not been able to develop new satisfying relationships and his/her loneliness is perpetual.

None of the above models of loneliness contradict each other. Each focuses on a different facet of loneliness. Taken together, we have a better understanding of how it is experienced and maintained in the lives of different people.

Summary

What is loneliness? It depends on how you look at it. We know that loneliness and social/emotional isolation are negative experiences, while solitude is a positive experience, and just being alone is neutral. The experience of loneliness is due to deficiencies in our social relationships and/or our perception of deficiencies in our relations.

There have been numerous studies to determine the antecedents of loneliness in people's lives. We may experience loneliness when there are changes in our social relationships, and/or changes in our social needs and desires. Loneliness also can occur as a result of traumatic events in our lives. Two of the more common sources of loneliness, however, are within ourselves—low self-esteem and negative self-image. These two factors may be combined with a lack of social skills. (Refer to chapter 3 for a more detailed study of self-esteem and its relationship to loneliness.)

The various models presented in this chapter looked at loneliness from different perspectives.

- The first considered loneliness in terms of *social and emotional needs*.
- The second made a distinction between *being alone and being lonely*.
- The third considered *different reactions to being lonely* and the results of those reactions.
- The final looked at the *duration* of the experience of loneliness as a way to define it.

Once again, if we put them all together, we have a good understanding of loneliness in general. At the same time, we can pick and choose the one or two that make the best sense to us in view of our personal experiences.

NOTES

[1]Letitia A. Peplau and Daniel Perlman, "Perspectives on Loneliness," in *Loneliness: A Source Book of Current Theory, Research and Therapy*, edited by Letitia A. Peplau and Daniel Perlman, (New York: John Wiley & Sons, 1982), pp. 1-20.

[2]Peplau and Perlman, pp. 3-6.

[3]Ami Rokach, "Antecedents of loneliness: A factorial analysis," *The Journal of Psychology*, Vol. 123, No. 4, p. 371.

[4]Rokach, p. 371.

[5]Rokach, p. 377.

[6]Robert Weiss, *Loneliness: The experience of emotional and social isolation*, (Cambridge, MA: MIT Press, 1973), p. 33.

[7]Clarke E. Moustakas, *Loneliness and Love*, (Englewood Cliffs, NJ: Prentice-Hall, 1972), pp. 19,21.

[8]Moustakas, p. 40.

[9]J. de Jong-Gierveld and J. Raadschelders, "Types of Loneliness," in *Loneliness: A Source Book of Current Theory, Research and Therapy*, edited by Letitia A. Peplau and Daniel Perlman, (New York: John Wiley & Sons, 1982), pp. 114-116.

[10]Jeffery Young, "Loneliness, Depression, and Cognitive Therapy: Theory and Application," in *Loneliness: A Source Book of Current Theory, Research and Therapy*, edited by Letitia A. Peplau and Daniel Perlman, (New York: John Wiley & Sons, 1982), p. 382.

CHAPTER 5:

A Relationship Perspective of Loneliness

Introduction

In chapter 2, we emphasized God's gracious relationship with us. In chapter 3, we considered ourselves as children of God. We focused on the individual Christian with a healthy self-esteem and suggested that such a healthy Christian self-esteem depends on our relationship with our gracious, understanding, and forgiving God. Chapter 4 considered the Scriptural and psychological aspects of loneliness.

In this chapter we will study loneliness from a relationship perspective. First, we will look at the connection between intimacy and loneliness. Following that, we will consider the different relationships in which we participate: the family of God, our marriage, our own family, and our friendships.

Intimacy and loneliness

Up front, we want to make this distinction: Intimacy is NOT to be equated with having sex! Sexual activity is a poor and often disastrous substitute for an intimate relationship. While sexual activity is meant to be a part of an intimate relationship between a husband and wife in a Christian marriage, sex and intimacy are not the same thing.

Carin Rubenstein and Phillip Shaver define intimacy as "a close personal relationship marked by . . . openness, honesty, mutual self-disclosure; caring, warmth, protecting, helping; being devoted to each other, mutually attentive, mutually committed; surrendering control, dropping defenses; becoming emotionally attached, feeling distressed when separation occurs."[1]

So how is intimacy connected to loneliness? Rubenstein and Shaver describe the relationship: "Just as hunger signals the body's need for nourishment, loneliness warns us that important psychological needs are going unmet. Loneliness is a healthy hunger for intimacy and community—a natural sign that we are lacking companionship, closeness, and a meaningful place in the world."[2]

> *Loneliness is a healthy hunger for intimacy and community—
> a natural sign that we are lacking companionship,
> closeness, and a meaningful place in the world.*

Our relationships do not all have the same level of intimacy. We simply feel closer to some people than we do to others. Rubenstein and Shaver place various types of relationships on an intimacy continuum from most intimate to least intimate. The most intimate relationships are those between spouses. The least intimate relationships are those with acquaintances. Between these two ends range the relationships between parent and child, between intimate friends, and between more distant friends and family members. The study of Rubenstein and Shaver distinguishes between intimacy and community. They characterize intimacy as a private sharing of one's self. They define community as one's public roles and responsibilities. Both are necessary for a healthy sense of well-being and belonging.

INTIMACY CONTINUUM

Most Intimate   Least Intimate

Spouse	Parent/ Child	Intimate Friend	Friends & Family	Acquaintances

In another study, Tim Timmons suggests that loneliness has "only one root cause: the absence of intimacy."[3] He suggests that intimacy is a sense of close attachment to another person. Such intimacy includes trust, confidentiality, and familiarity. We might say that intimacy measures the degree to which we share our "self" with another person. In a truly intimate relationship, this sharing is mutual. Both individuals open themselves to each other because they are motivated by a true love for one another.

Valerian Derlega and Stephen Margulis present another view of intimacy describing it as "a social form of privacy in the sense that it brings individuals together in open communication."[4] In a private, intimate relationship, we may be quite open with our self-disclosure, such as, what we tell another person about our personal thoughts, feelings, and experiences. In our relationships, we expect our partner to be equally open with us. When our partner does not meet this expectation of mutual sharing or when the partner betrays our trust, the result will be a sense of loneliness.

Timmons also notes this risk: "Yet the very place of safety that an intimate relationship provides has with it the potential for causing deep feelings of loneliness. That is the risk of intimacy."[5] King David expressed such a wounding of intimacy in Psalm 55:12-14. "If an enemy were insulting me, I could endure it; if a foe were raising himself against me, I could hide from him. But it is you, a man like myself, my companion, my close friend, with whom I once enjoyed sweet fellowship." To have lost such an intimate relationship or to never have had such an intimate relationship is truly a lonely experience, from which one does not quickly recover.

Intimate relationships are developed through interpersonal communication. As individuals, we set boundaries for ourselves as to how much of our "self" we are willing to reveal to another person. Derlega and Margulis found that people who tend to be lonely may not understand how to set appropriate boundaries for their self-disclosure. They may reveal too much about themselves too soon in a relationship, which may scare away others. Or, fearing the vulnerability of intimacy, they may build communication barriers between themselves and all others—including the people they want to love. In so doing they isolate themselves socially. In order to develop a healthy, intimate relationship with another person, it is important for us to set appropriate boundaries for our self-disclosures.

To illustrate this concept, picture yourself as an onion. An onion has many layers of skin that can be peeled away to get to its heart. We can peel off a single layer of skin from around the entire onion (breadth), or we can take a knife and cut a wedge deep into the onion (depth). In essence, the breadth is the quantity of our self-disclosure—how many different topics we want to discuss. The depth is the quality of our self-disclosure—how much of our self we want to reveal on any given topic.

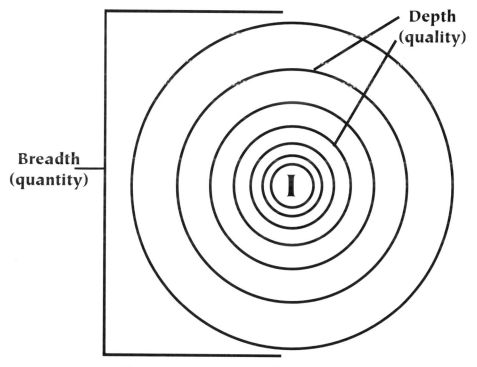

The Onion Analogy of Self-Disclosure

In our communication with others,
we select how much personal information
we want them to know.

The Social Penetration model (Altman and Taylor) points out that in our communication with others, we select how much personal information we want them to know. For example, when we first meet a person and are making small talk about sports and weather, we reveal only a surface layer of our "onion" about several topics. On the other hand, we may reveal all we know—all our thoughts and all our feelings—to a person about a single topic, cutting a deep but narrow wedge into our "onion." We do this when we talk with a doctor about a health matter. In still another situation, we may reveal much of our thoughts, feelings, and experiences related to many areas of our life, cutting several thick slices from our "onion." We do this when we confide in a close friend or spouse. The relationship, the situation, and the purpose of the communication all help us to decide what is the appropriate breadth and depth of self-disclosure.[6]

God wants us to be truthful with one another about our thoughts and feelings because this is the only way that fulfilling relationships can grow. However, he does not tell us that we have to tell everything to everybody we meet. We only need to disclose what is helpful for building up each other and the relationship according to our mutual needs.

The concept of intimacy helps us understand that the quality of a relationship is more important than the number, or quantity, of relationships. A person who has many surface relationships or many acquaintances and is active in many organizations, but who desires and lacks an intimate relationship, probably will experience loneliness. On the other hand, a person in a loving, intimate relationship may have few outside acquaintances and activities and yet be content. However, should that person lose that relationship, his/her loneliness probably will be intense.

With this understanding of intimacy in relationships and its effect on loneliness, let us consider various relationships in which we participate. We will begin with our membership in the family of God. Then we will consider the relationships of marriage, family, and friends.

The family of God

The apostle Paul describes the family of God as the spiritual body of Christ in 1 Corinthians 12:12-27:

The body is a unit, though it is made up of many parts; and though all its parts are many, they form one body. So it is with Christ. For we were all baptized by one Spirit into one body—whether Jews of Greeks, slave or free—and we were all given the one Spirit to drink. Now the body is not made up of one part but of many. If the foot should say, "Because I am not a hand, I do not belong to the body," it would not for that reason cease to be part of the body. . . . But in fact God has arranged the parts in the body, every one of them, just as he wanted them to be. . . . The eye cannot say to the hand, "I don't need you!" And the head cannot say to the feet, "I don't need you!" . . . But God has combined the members of the body and has given greater honor to the parts that lacked it, so that there should be no division in the body, but that its parts should have equal concern for each other. If one parts suffers, every part suffers with it; if one part is honored, every part rejoices with it. Now you are the body of Christ, and each one of you is a part of it.

As God intended it, the family of God provides an opportunity for every member to have healthy self-esteem, a sense of belonging and community, and intimacy without fear of vulnerability. We are united by the Holy Spirit in the love of Christ. We share a common faith and a common goal—the salvation of our souls. The Holy Spirit has given each one of us the necessary gifts so that we can be effective contributing members to the common good of the family. Notice that not all the gifts are the same just as not all Christians are the same.

God brought us into his family on this earth
to help one another.
This sense of belonging and having equal concern
for one another implies a mutual sharing of self
for the common good.

God brought us into his family on this earth to help one another. This sense of belonging and having equal concern for one another implies a mutual sharing of self for the common good. In Romans 12:5, the apostle Paul added this thought: "So in Christ we who are many form one body, and each member belongs to all the others." In times of sorrow and suffering, we are to support one another. In times of happiness and prosperity, we are to rejoice with one another. In order to know when we are to mourn and when we are to rejoice with one another, we need to communicate openly with the other members of Christ's body. We can risk self-disclosure with other members of God's family without fear of betrayal because Christ in love brought us together. We realize that we need each other. Although each one of us is independent, yet we carrying each others burdens. As Paul writes in Galatians 6:2, "Carry each other's burdens, and in this way you will fulfill the law of Christ."

God brought us into his family on this earth
to help one another.

It's a beautiful painting, isn't it? Yet in the real world, one flaw mars the canvass—sin. In our sinfulness, we do not fulfill the law of Christ. Because the family of God is made up of sinners, we have become afraid to be intimate with our fellow Christians. Our own sin and the sin of others blocks our attempts at intimate relationships with other Christians. When people at church ask us, "How are you doing?" we put on our "church face," smile, and reply, "Fine!"

This creates a sad downward spiral in our communications with fellow members of the family of God. When we see so many people smiling and doing "fine," we are led to believe that we are the only lonely people in our congregation. We begin to think that it would be terrible of us to "burden" the others with our problems. And so we keep it all to ourselves and continue in our misery and loneliness among the very people God intended for us to have as our intimate friends and family. What a tragedy!

What can we do about it? Several things are possible. *If we are lonely*, it requires that we take the risk of vulnerability and communicate with a fellow Christian. We need to choose this person wisely, perhaps even asking our pastor to help us with that choice. Then, with their permission, we begin to share our thoughts, feelings, and experiences—slowly peeling our onion ever more widely and deeply. We may fail at times and endure disappointment, but we need to continue to make the effort, perhaps with a new friend.

God works within us through the gospel
in Word and sacrament, empowering us to live as he desires,
whether we are lonely and in need of a friend or
not lonely and can become a friend.

If we are not lonely, we can be helpful. We encounter many lonely people in our circle of fellow Christians. We need to be sensitive to them. If we suspect that someone is a lonely person, we are required to take the risk of rejection and communicate with that person. We will sincerely ask how they are doing and take the time to listen to their answer. Through our responses, we will give them permission to let down their "church face" and open up to us. If you choose to do this, remember that you need to be ready and willing to mourn with those who mourn and to suffer with those who suffer. But isn't this what God intended for his family members to do for one another?

In both cases, the effort requires the spiritual strength that believers in Christ find in the gospel. For the lonely, taking the risk of vulnerability comes from knowing that Christ loves them unconditionally and forgives every sin. For the non-lonely, the ability to listen and to help comes from knowing that Christ's love is for all and that they can show his compassion to others. No spiritual strength comes to believers except through the means of grace. God works within us through the gospel in Word and sacrament, empowering us to live as he desires, whether we are lonely and in need of a friend or not lonely and can become a friend.

Marriage

There is a common misconception that marriage is the answer to loneliness. In fact, this misconception is so widespread that many lonely wives and husbands are embarrassed to reveal their loneliness. They think it is illogical and socially unacceptable.

There is a common misconception
that marriage is the answer to loneliness.

Dan Kiley notes that wives report loneliness more often than husbands do. He found that such loneliness tends to occur after ten years of marriage when the woman is around 35 years of age and is married to a self-involved husband. The woman often is well-educated, is apparently successful as a wife and mother, and is socially active. She may also have a successful professional career. So why is she lonely? Because, in the one relationship in which she is desiring and expecting intimacy, there is none. The result is emotional isolation and a sense of inadequacy and failure. Husbands experience similar loneliness, although perhaps not as frequently.[7]

For Christian spouses, the tragedy of this "living together in loneliness," as Kiley speaks of it, is that God intended otherwise. Consider just three of the marriage passages in the Bible:

> Wives, submit to your husbands as to the Lord. For the husband is the head of the wife as Christ is the head of the church, his body, of which he is the Savior. Now as the church submits to Christ, so also wives should submit to their husbands in everything. Husbands, love your wives, just as Christ loved the church and gave himself up for her. . . . In this same way, husbands ought to love their wives as their own bodies. He who loves his wife loves himself. After all, no one ever hated his own body, but he feeds and cares for it, just as Christ does the church—for we are members of his body. "For this reason a man will leave his father and mother and be united to his wife, and the two will become one flesh." (Ephesians 5:22-31)

Sadly, most people stop reading this passage two words into verse 22, "Wives, submit." In doing so, we lose sight of God's admonition to Christian husbands. Husbands are to be "heads" as Christ is our Head—coming to serve rather than to be served. Husbands are to give themselves up for their wives, as Christ gave himself up for us. Husbands are to love and care for their wives as they would themselves. In response to such self-giving love, wives are to submit lovingly and willingly to their husbands, just as the church willingly submits in loving response to our self-giving Savior.

Please note that the concepts "to give self up for" and "to submit," as presented in Scripture, can be understood only in the light of the love of Christ. To give oneself up for another is an act of loving service out of consideration for the needs of another. It is not to be confused with "giving in" to another, which implies coercion in a win-lose situation. To submit is also a willful, loving act as opposed to a forced, fearful capitulation. A wife willingly submits to her husband out of love for him, as he lovingly gives himself up for her.

> Wives, submit to your husbands, as is fitting in the Lord. Husbands, love your wives and do not be harsh with them. (Colossians 3:18,19)

Christian wives are to submit to their husbands as is fitting in the Lord. In other words, such submission is to be in obedience to God. Thus, if a husband demands something of a wife that is not God-pleasing, the wife is not required to submit. In view of this, God admonishes Christian husbands not to be harsh with their wives. This eliminates any form of abusive behavior, whether it is emotional, verbal, physical, or sexual abuse. Husbands are to live with their wives in self-giving love rather than in self-gratifying domination.

> Wives, in the same way be submissive to your husbands . . . Husbands, in the same way be considerate as you live with your wives, and treat them with respect as the weaker partner and as heirs with you of the gracious gift of life, so that nothing will hinder your prayers. (1 Peter 3:1-7)

In this final marriage passage, God calls upon Christian husbands to live with their wives in consideration and with respect for them as their partners in marriage, and as fellow children of God. When we read these passages and others, we come to appreciate the balance and interdependence God established for husband and wife in marriage.

Therefore if Christian husbands and wives would live together in the love of Christ as God has intended for them, would there be loneliness in Christian marriages? Sadly, therein is the tragedy of many Christian marriages. Sinfulness keeps one or both spouses from fulfilling God's plan for husbands and wives. God willing, two Christians can work together in the love of Christ and in response to the Word of God to renew or establish intimacy in their marriage. The power to act as Christians within marriage comes from God. Wives learn the meaning of submission for their own lives as they learn how every Christian submits to Christ. Husbands learn to love as they learn how deeply Christ loved them and all sinners. God provides the strength to live according to his will through the means of grace, the gospel in Word and sacrament. Without that power, Christians cannot overcome any spiritual problem and have no spiritual strength to overcome problems in any relationship.

Loneliness in marriage does not need to be a permanent condition. If your spouse is not willing to change his or her behavior in response to God's Word, seek counseling from your pastor and/or a professional Christian counselor. There are answers and solutions available, if you are willing to take the risk of change and seek the help you need.

Loneliness in marriage does not need to be a permanent condition.

Perhaps *the relationship itself can change*. However, it requires both partners to accomplish this type of change. Such a change will require communication, patience, and prayer. Many times a counselor can help to reestablish an appropriate pattern of communication. Once that is accomplished, both will be able to work at improvement and to discuss the process openly and constructively.

If both partners are not ready to work for change, maybe *one partner can make changes* in his or her part in the relationship. For example, if you desire to change your pattern, watch for "triggers," those things that your spouse does or says that "set you off." Instead of reacting in anger or bitterness that may serve only to make the situation worse, try these three strategies:

1. Stop and think before you speak, pout, cry, or yell.
2. Speak calmly and express your thoughts or feelings without attacking your spouse as a person.
3. If he/she still wants to argue, excuse yourself and walk away.

If you see no change in your spouse, at least you will feel better about your behavior and contribution to the relationship. This is only one suggestion. There are many more ways to change your part in the relationship.

Changing the expectations of the relationship can also be helpful. By this we do not mean that anyone gives up hope, or denies the dreams for the relationship, or lowers the goals for the relationship. The idea is for one partner to bring his or her expectations of the partner's behavior into line with reality. For instance, continue to hope that someday your spouse will understand and have dinner started when you get home; but for today, before you walk in the front door, remind yourself that you expect nothing to be started. Then, if it is started, it will be a pleasant surprise. If not, your spouse will only have met your expectations, and your level of disappointment and frustration will be lower.

Family (parent and child)

Several relationships fall within the context of family. The first is that of husband and wife, which we have covered under marriage. The second is the relationship between parent and child. The third is that of siblings, or brothers and sisters. We will focus on the parent/child relationship here. The relationship of brothers and sisters will come up later in this section. As we concentrate on the parent and child, we note that this relationship is especially important to the child's development as an individual in later years. The Bible tells us in Proverbs 22:6, "Train a child in the way he should go, and when he is old he will not turn from it."

Mother-child attachment begins in the womb. During the nine months of gestation a bond grows between mother and child. That little baby is not just a part of the mother's body. That baby is a new person growing within the mother's body. Mothers generally feel the excitement of feeling the new life beginning to move within them. During the pregnancy, mother and child get to know one another as the baby develops and grows. The mother begins to share her life with this person.

When there is a miscarriage, an abortion, or a stillbirth, grief and loneliness occur, especially for the mother. Often, the mother goes through a time of guilt and questioning; she wonders what she did to cause the death. At such a time, she needs emotional support. Instead, she may only hear, "Don't worry, you can still have another one." The father should be sensitive to his wife's emotional need for support, as well as to the questions of other members of the family.

We don't tell children to sit down with a book and paper

and write out the answers to life and relationships.

We show them and serve as their examples

as we walk along the road or

take care of things around the house.

Unsympathetic responses do not allow the mother to grieve for the lost child and the lost dreams. Her grief and loneliness may be repressed if the only advice she receives is a rather matter-of-fact, "You just have to get on with your life." It is important to give not only the mother but also the father and siblings time and permission to grieve for the lost baby. One way to do this is to give the baby a name and talk about how it would have been to raise this child. Such personalization of the baby allows for a healing of the grief and loneliness. It also reduces the chances of the next child becoming the "replacement" child, who often is either overprotected or never quite good enough.

When God gives a child to parents, he expects a positive relationship to develop. According to God's plan, the relationship between parent and child provides an opportunity to nurture the child's mind, body, heart, and soul. Parents are to be teachers and models for their children in both earthly and heavenly matters. Because young children tend to learn mostly by observation, parental teaching is, more often than not, informal. We don't tell children to sit down with a book and paper and write out the answers to life and relationships. We show them and serve as their examples as we walk along the road or take care of things around the house.

As Christian parents, we want our children to learn more than just the knowledge of the world. We want them to be made "wise for salvation through faith in Christ Jesus" (2 Timothy 3:15). Thus Christian parents are feeding not only the bodies and minds of their children, but also their souls. That's what God wants.

> Hear, O Israel: The LORD our God, the LORD is one. Love the LORD your God with all your heart and with all your soul and with all your strength. These commandments that I give you today are to be upon your hearts. Impress them on your children. Talk about them when you sit at home and when you walk along the road, when you lie down and when you get up. (Deuteronomy 6:4-7)

Finally, how we parents express our own emotions, especially our happiness, sadness, love, and anger, becomes the classroom in which our children learn to identify and express their emotions to others. Is our style of communication God-pleasing? Do we let "unwholesome talk come out of [our] mouths" (Ephesians 4:29)? Do we discipline in love or in anger (James 1:19,20)? By our own communication styles, do we teach our children to treat each other with gentleness and respect? Do we teach them to say from their hearts: "I love you." "Please." "Thank you." "I'm sorry." and "I forgive you."? The best way to teach the commandments of God is by living them in the love of Christ.

The Lord calls upon mothers and fathers to be actively involved in their children's growth and development. Such involvement leads to a healthy attachment between parents and children. This, in turn, leads to a healthy sense of self-esteem and self-worth within the children. Such attitudes reduce the child's chances to experience loneliness.

In such a nurturing parent/child relationship, the children

1) become aware of their relationship with a loving heavenly Father and Savior, and

2) develop a sense of security and belonging in a loving family atmosphere.

Psychologically speaking, the child's social needs are met at all levels—spiritual, emotional, physical, and mental. This greatly reduces the chances of the child experiencing loneliness within the family context.

The Lord calls upon mothers and fathers to be actively involved in their children's growth and development. . . . Psychologically speaking, the child's social needs are met at all levels— spiritual, emotional, physical, and mental.

From the child's perspective, the family relationship is different. But here too there are always two sides to every relationship. Notice how the following passages impress upon children their responsibility to obey, but they also speak to parents, especially fathers, about their responsibilities toward their children.

- Children, obey your parents in the Lord, for this is right. "Honor your father and mother"—which is the first commandment with a promise—"that it may go well with you and that you may enjoy long life on the earth." Fathers, do not exasperate your children; instead, bring them up in the training and instruction of the Lord. (Ephesians 6:1-4)

- Children, obey your parents in everything, for this pleases the Lord. Fathers, do not embitter your children, or they will become discouraged. (Colossians 3:20,21)

Children are called upon to obey their parents in the Lord as a way of honoring them as God's representatives. A child's obedience to parents is an important way of showing obedience to God. This implies that the requests or commands of the parents are God-pleasing. Therefore parents are commanded to not exasperate or discourage their children.

Parents often exasperate and discourage their children through their lack of emotional involvement with their children. Another way is through their inconsistency (1) in their own behaviors in relation to their commands (i.e., Do as I say, not as I do), and (2) in their discipline patterns. Parents may use double standards, show favoritism, fail to follow through on consequences, or find fault instead of giving encouragement and praise for effort. A parent's lack of emotional involvement and consistency increases the sense of insecurity within the child. The child is uncertain of how he or she can contribute to and belong in the family. The result of this confusion is often discouragement and loneliness for the child.

In God's plan, the parent/child relationship
is meant to lead toward separation.

In God's plan, the parent/child relationship is meant to lead toward separation. God says, "For this reason a man will leave his father and mother and be united to his wife, and they will become one flesh" (Genesis 2:24). Christian parents train their children to make God-pleasing decisions, including that of choosing a lifelong mate and beginning a new family away from Mom and Dad.

As the children leave the home, mother especially may experience the empty nest syndrome. She may experience a major change in her role. When the children are no longer under the same roof, she and her husband will be alone together. If they have not maintained a healthy, growing husband/wife relationship over the last 20 to 30 years, they may find that they have little in common. Their social, interpersonal needs and expectations are no longer met by one another. Although both may experience loneliness, it is usually the wife who experiences it with greater intensity.

Josh McDowell and Norm Wakefield identify another type of emptiness that is prevalent today in American culture. Children often come home after school to empty houses. Both parents are away at work. Younger children have a natural desire to share the news of their day with Mom and Dad. They want to tell of the exciting things that happened during the day, and they want to be comforted about the bad things in their day. When no one is home, this desire is unfulfilled, resulting in a sense of loneliness.[8]

Because both parents are often required to work today to make ends meet, this situation is going to occur. Being at home when the children return is not always possible. Thus it is important to compensate for that on a daily basis, so that the child knows that he or she is loved and "belongs." It is important for parents to take time when they come home to seek out the child and review their day together.

Divorce. One last source of loneliness within the family that is becoming more prevalent in our society today is divorce. There is the loneliness and grieving experienced by the divorced spouse. There is also the loneliness and grieving experienced by the children.

In family counseling, we try to instill in parents the idea that children need to see them as one—"MomandDad." This gives the family a sense of consistency, stability, and safety. In divorce, this often becomes "Momand . . . Dad" or "Mom . . . andDad." The children are forced to make choices they do not want to make. One important person in their life is no longer present. It is unfair and unrealistic to expect the remaining parent to take on the roles of both parents. The "rules" say that children are supposed to leave their parents, not the other way around. In the confusion and inconsistency created by this parental void, the children experience loneliness.

The relationship between child and parent changes as parents grow older. When the children were young, parents provided the nurture and support for their children. As parents grow older, they may have a greater need for social, financial, emotional, and physical support. God looks to the children and grandchildren to provide this support. It is a matter of Christian faith; it is not an option. Eventually a time comes when children and grandchildren repay the parents. Consider 1 Timothy 5:3-8:

> If a widow has children or grandchildren, these should learn first of all to put their religion into practice by caring for their own family and so repaying their parents and grandparents, for this is pleasing to God. . . . If anyone does not provide for his relatives, and especially for his immediate family, he has denied the faith and is worse than an unbeliever.

The need for social and emotional attachment is a lifelong need.

Although the elderly as a group are among the least lonely, they still need family contact. They need a sense of belonging, a sense of family that says someone cares. Even though they may protest that they do not want to be a burden to anybody, without this sense of attachment, loneliness will result. The need for social and emotional attachment is a lifelong need.

Family (siblings)

In their study among the elderly, Larry Mullins and Elizabeth Dugan found that brothers and sisters have a unique lifelong relationship. Siblings are often fairly close in age and share many common childhood experiences. Over a lifetime, brothers and sisters provide each other with ties to family history and tradition.[9] Little research has been done as to how continued sibling contact affects loneliness. In this section we will look at the experiences of Joseph and his brothers and draw some lessons from their relationship.

The biblical family of Joseph and his brothers gives us one example of sibling relationships. Early in Joseph's life, an intense sibling rivalry developed with his other brothers.

Jacob, their father, made matters worse by showing favoritism toward Joseph by providing a special coat for him. The rivalry erupted one day when Joseph was sent to check on his brothers. The brothers sold Joseph and told their father that he had been killed by a wild animal.

Siblings are often fairly close in age and share many common childhood experiences. Over a lifetime, brothers and sisters provide each other with ties to family history and tradition.

While Joseph was separated from his brothers, God was with him throughout his time of slavery and imprisonment. The Lord took him from a prison cell to the second most powerful office in Egypt—second only to the pharaoh. Nevertheless, these years were a time of emotional and social isolation for Joseph, in that he was cut off from his family by the jealous actions of his brothers. Joseph did find a satisfying marriage and had two sons. But he was still absent from his extended family.

When the Lord brought his brothers to Egypt to seek food, we see evidence of Joseph's loneliness—his emotional and social need to be with his family. In the following passages, we also see an example of the notion that it is not the quantity but rather the quality of a relationship that counts. Joseph's stepbrothers were all present, but the one he really wanted to see was Benjamin, the only other son of his mother. In Genesis 43:29,30 we read:

> As he looked about and saw his brother Benjamin, his own mother's son, he asked, "Is this your youngest brother, the one you told me about?" And he said, "God be gracious to you, my son." Deeply moved at the sight of his brother, Joseph hurried out and looked for a place to weep. He went into his private room and wept there.

Even though Joseph's family was now in his presence, he was still experiencing isolation from his father and brothers because he had not yet revealed himself to them. Joseph tested his brothers to see if they still possessed the rivalry that led them to sell him as a slave. When he discovered that it was gone, Genesis 45:1-11 tells us:

> Then Joseph could no longer control himself before all his attendants, and he cried out, "Have everyone leave my presence!" So there was no one with Joseph when he made himself known to his brothers. And he wept so loudly that the Egyptians heard him, and Pharaoh's household heard about it. Joseph said to his brothers, "I am Joseph! Is my father still living?" But his brothers were not able to answer him, because they were terrified at his presence. Then Joseph said to his brothers, "Come close to me." When they had done so, he said, "I am your brother Joseph, the one you sold into Egypt! And now, do not be distressed and do not be angry with yourselves for selling me here, because it was to save lives that God sent me ahead of you. . . . Now hurry back to my father and say to him, 'This is what your son Joseph says: God has made me lord of all Egypt. Come down to me; don't delay. You shall live in the region of Goshen and be near me—you, your children and grandchildren, your flocks and herds, and all you have. I will provide for you there, because five years of famine are still to come. Otherwise you and your household and all who belong to you will become destitute.'"

Not only do we see Joseph's emotional and social needs and desires being fulfilled by renewed contact with his family, we also see the wondrous healing power of God's grace in Joseph's heart. Estranged from his family by his brothers' jealous and hateful acts years earlier, Joseph does not hold a grudge against them. He puts an end to his years of loneliness—a loneliness experienced while he was the most important and popular man in all of Egypt.

Friends

As noted earlier, it is neither the number of friendships nor the frequency of contact with friends that has an effect on loneliness. Rather, loneliness depends more on the quality of a relationship and the individual's satisfaction with that relationship. In light of this, we might say that a lonely person who goes out and joins numerous clubs and organizations and makes many acquaintances may possibly end up being a highly active lonely person.[10]

Neither the number of friendships

nor the frequency of contact with friends . . .

has an effect on loneliness.

Rather, loneliness depends more on the quality

of a relationship and the individual's satisfaction

with that relationship.

In his study of friendships and loneliness among children, Zick Rubin found that a lack of social skills often had an affect on children's ability to establish close friendships. These social skills included the abilities to "gain entry into group activities, to be approving and supportive to their peers, to manage conflicts appropriately, and to exercise sensitivity and tact."[11] Rubin also noted that children needed to be attentive and considerate toward others in order for friendships to be formed. Children who tended to be more self-focused and less cooperative often were without close friends.

Josh McDowell and Norm Wakefield described four types of disappointing friendships:

1) part-time friendships
2) conditional friendships
3) undependable friendships
4) superficial friendships

Part-time friends are mostly acquaintances, that is, people you may know in a group setting but with whom you share no personal interests. Conditional friends offer friendships in return for conformity to their rules, needs, and desires. Undependable friends are careless with your friendship. They may betray confidences or act irresponsibly when you are in need of their presence and support. Finally, superficial friends rarely, if ever, take you or the relationship seriously. When you try to take a conversation to a deeper level, they change the subject or keep it at a surface level. Having such friendships can still leave us with a sense of loneliness because our expectations for the relationships are not being fulfilled.

A close friendship involves a mutual sharing
of oneself with another. . . .
A close friendship is built on
mutual love, trust, and acceptance.

In the above examples of disappointing friendships, the one thing that was missing was *the intimacy of a close friendship*. A close friendship involves a mutual sharing of oneself with another. This sharing of self includes our ideas, our feelings, our interests, our faith, our bad times and good times. It involves being there for one another—giving and receiving support in time of need. A close friendship is built on mutual love, trust, and acceptance.

In his book *Intimate Connections*, David Burns had an interesting thought. He found that in order to overcome loneliness it was important to develop a sense of healthy self-esteem. In order to do this, he suggested that lonely people first learn how to be alone and discover themselves before seeking to establish close relationships. The idea is that when we enjoy and appreciate ourselves, we believe that we have something to offer a relationship. This allows us to become intimate because we see ourselves as being someone worth sharing with another, which is the essence of any close relationship.[12]

The Bible gives us several examples of the various patterns of friendship. David and Jonathan shared a close friendship (cf. 1 Samuel 18–20). Jonathan loved David as himself and held their friendship more dear than his relationship with his own father. When separated by Saul's hatred for David, they experienced loneliness in one another's absence.

Whereas Jesus gave his disciples unconditional, full-time, dependable, and meaningful friendship, they often disappointed him. They betrayed him (Judas); they denied him (Peter); they ran away from him (at his arrest); and they were not there for him when he needed their support and prayers in the Garden of Gethsemane. Jesus had firsthand experience with loneliness due to disappointing friendships.

Summary

In this review of the relationship perspective of loneliness, we have seen that intimacy is the essential ingredient to a fulfilling and satisfying relationship—whether it be in a marriage, within a family, or between friends. It was also noted that in order to become intimate with another person, we need to have two important factors: (1) a healthy sense of self-esteem, and (2) adequate social skills.

Intimacy is the essential ingredient to a fulfilling and satisfying relationship.

Within the family of God, we have opportunity to develop a healthy Christian self-esteem. The body of Christ is based on the concept of mutual respect and concern for one another. In this spiritual and social atmosphere, motivated by the grace of God in Christ, intimate relationships can grow. The Ten Commandments, the two great commandments, and other directives from the Bible (Ephesians 4:25-32; Philippians 2:1-5; Colossians 3) teach us the necessary skills for healthy, intimate relationships among family members and between friends in the love of Christ. God's gracious forgiveness in Christ provides the motivation to live as God asks. God works within us as we hear, read, and remember the message of his redeeming love for us.

In chapter 6, we will view loneliness along the life cycle from a developmental perspective. We will consider loneliness among children, adolescents, young adults, and elder adults.

NOTES

[1] Carin Rubenstein and Phillip Shaver, *In Search of Intimacy*, (New York: Delacorte Press, 1982), p. 21.

[2] Rubenstein and Shaver, p. 3.

[3] Tim Timmons, *Loneliness Is Not a Disease*, (New York: Ballentine, 1981), p. 10.

[4] Valerian Derlega and Stephen Margulis, "Why Loneliness Occurs: The Interrelationship of Social-psychological and Privacy Concepts," in *Loneli-*

ness: A Source Book of Current Theory, Research and Therapy, edited by Letitia A. Peplau and Daniel Perlman, (New York: John Wiley & Sons, 1982), p. 159.

[5]Timmons, p. 111.

[6]Irwin Altman and Dalmas A. Taylor, Social Penetration: The Development of Interpersonal Relationships, (New York: Holt, Rinehart & Winston, 1973).

[7]Dan Kiley, Living Together, Feeling Alone, (New York: Prentice Hall Press, 1989).

[8]Josh McDowell and Norm Wakefield, Friend of the Lonely Heart, (Dallas: Word, 1991).

[9]Larry Mullins and Elizabeth Dugan, "The Influence of Depression, and Family and Friendship Relations on Residents' Loneliness in Congregate Housing," in The Gerontologist, Vol. 30, No. 3, 1990, pp. 377-384.

[10]Warren Jones, "Loneliness and Social Behavior," in Loneliness: A Source Book of Current Theory, Research and Therapy, edited by Letitia A. Peplau and Daniel Perlman, (New York: John Wiley & Sons, 1982), pp. 238-252.

[11]Zick Rubin, "Children Without Friends." in Loneliness: A Source Book of Current Theory, Research and Therapy, edited by Letitia A. Peplau and Daniel Perlman, (New York: John Wiley & Sons, 1982), pp. 256,257.

[12]David Burns, Intimate Connections, (New York: Morrow, 1985).

CHAPTER 6:

Developmental Perspective of Loneliness

Introduction

In the previous chapter, we looked at loneliness from the perspective of relationships (family of God, marriage, family, and friends). In this chapter, we consider the possible sources of loneliness throughout life. We begin with childhood, move on to adolescence, early adulthood, middle adulthood, and finish with late adulthood. It may surprise some that late adulthood (over 60) is NOT the loneliest time of life. Research shows that adolescents are the most susceptible to loneliness. It is also a common misconception to think that little children are "resilient" and do not experience loneliness.

Childhood

After up to nine months of intimate attachment to his or her mother, a newborn child bursts into the light of an unfriendly world. The womb was a place of safety, closeness, warmth, familiarity, and peace. The baby's first experience is separation from all that is familiar. Then comes a reunion with the one person in this new world that the infant knows intimately— Mom—as she cuddles her newborn baby in her loving arms.

So begins a child's journey into life—a life that will be filled with numerous attachments, separations, and loneliness. Children are precious gifts of God. In Psalm 127:3 we read, "Sons are a heritage from the LORD, children a reward from him." God loans these precious little ones to parents, so that they may care for them, nurture them, and raise them in the instruction of the Lord to become responsible adult children of God. Much of what we learn about life, we learn in early childhood as we observe and interact with our parents.

Much of what we learn about life,
we learn in early childhood
as we observe and interact with our parents.

John Killinger noted that "[Children] need the feel of flesh upon flesh, the sense of the mother's warm presence, the sound of her loving voice. This is the source of their security. . . . The need children have for their mothers immediately after birth does not suddenly go away when they are six months or a year old. It continues with little abatement through the first three years of their lives."[1]

As young toddlers begin to boldly and tentatively venture out into their environment to discover their new world and themselves, they need that sense of attachment and security that has been developed in infancy since conception. Toddlers feel secure during these brief moments of separation from their parents, provided they can quickly return at will to their safe haven. It is a game of "Mommy, I'm leaving you, but don't you leave me." Young children, whose early attachment needs have not been met in infancy, will be more sensitive to separation and, thus, more vulnerable to loneliness.

Little children tend to assign a spirit of life—
and thus an emotional attachment—to inanimate objects
and special places in their personal world.

Another source of loneliness for young children can be a separation from objects or places. The potential for loneliness comes when the family must move. Little children tend to assign a spirit of life—and thus an emotional attachment—to inanimate objects and special places in their personal world. When children are forced to leave these behind, they are losing some dear friends. This may lead to an experience of emotional isolation. It is important for parents to be aware of this attachment to inanimate objects in their children's lives and not to minimize its importance to their children. During the emotional distress of a move, children do not need to hear a cold, "Forget about it; it's just a stuffed bear. You can get another one at our new house." We need to give them understanding and a time to grieve over their losses. We must also understand the child's attachment to their own special places. Perhaps parents can encourage them to say farewell to the old and explore new special places in the new home.

As children enter into *middle childhood* and *preadolescence,* a natural separation process begins to take place. These older children identify more and more with their peer groups than with their parents. Their buddies and friends take on more importance to them. This is a healthy part of the maturation process. However, parents need to remember that they are still very important to their children's emotional and social development at this time. Children still need that "safe haven" to return to for reality checks and for the setting of reasonable boundaries.

As children enter into middle childhood and preadolescence, a natural separation process begins to take place.

Belonging to "the group" is important during these years. Children who have not learned the necessary social skills in their earlier years of playing with their siblings and other children in their neighborhood or in day care and preschool may be at a disadvantage socially. They may not know how to initiate entrance into groups. This leaves them with a sense of social isolation. It is important for parents to be aware of a child's social development. Parents should always offer their children emotional support and, at times, they may need to help them learn the social skills they may be lacking.

When older children move into a new area or attend a new school, it is often difficult for them to break into the already established group circles. There is a natural fear of rejection, combined with a sense of grief over the loss of previous friends. An older child may think, "I'll never have another friend like Chris!" Such a fear may inhibit a smooth transition to a new circle of friends and acquaintances. Once again, parents play an important role in offering their children understanding and support at such times. Parents need to be especially careful not to minimize the importance of this problem in the lives of their children.

Becoming involved as a family with groups at church, school, and work can ease these transitional difficulties. Taking time to become acquainted with the new neighbors as a family is also helpful. The children may respond, "Oh, Mom! Oh, Dad!" to a parent's efforts to integrate the family into new surroundings, but these opportunities for social contact with different peer groups are valuable. They allow the children to once again move away from their parents into new groups at their own pace. Children at any age need a sense of belonging and community.

> *Group conformity is essential to children of this age, and the standards for conformity are totally subjective to those within the group.*

Even when they are among friends, children can experience emotional or social isolation and loneliness. There can be an emphasis on group popularity among children of this age. A child's "friend" today may be someone else's "friend" tomorrow. It takes only a nasty word or rumor from one of the "in group" and suddenly a child is on the outside, looking in. Social competition can be fierce and painful for the losers.

Group conformity is essential to children of this age, and the standards for conformity are totally subjective to those within the group.

As much as we may wish it were not so, physical attractiveness and/or athletic ability are of high importance in our society. If a child is not pretty enough, handsome enough, or talented enough to meet a certain group's standard of acceptance, that child will experience a sense of rejection and social isolation. Self-image will be wounded. Rejection may lead a child to feel isolated and lonely.

It is important throughout childhood for parents to appreciate their children as individual children of God (see chapter 3). Children who have experienced acceptance as individuals within the home, who have had a chance to appreciate and utilize the gifts God has given to them that make them unique, will have a sense of self-acceptance as well. It will not make the rejection any less painful at the time, but the recovery will be quicker, because they will realize that their self-worth does not depend on the subjective opinions of others. These children will be better equipped to develop friendships within groups that have similar interests and values to their own, rather than believing they must either "be in" or "be dead."

Adolescence

During the teen years, adolescents experience a time of self-identification and self-discovery. In some ways, this time is similar to the toddler years. It is a time of ever-increasing separation and independence from parents. The need for good social skills is even more important in the high school years. It is a time of change at all levels—social, physical, sexual, emotional, and relational. For parents and teens alike, it can be a time of mutual enjoyment and mutual frustration. It is also a time of high—some say highest—vulnerability to loneliness.

Research shows that adolescents
are the most susceptible to loneliness.

At times adolescents are children trying to act like adults. At times they are adults acting like children. In either case, they are acting their age—an age of transition from late childhood into early adulthood. Their primary developmental purpose is to establish an identity of self founded on what they have learned as children and what they are presently discovering in their world. It is a time of growing out of primarily group-oriented relationships into more personal relationships, especially with the opposite sex. It is a time of confusion, questions, and doubts about themselves, about what they have been and are learning, and about their own place in the world.

When the teens are vocally claiming independence and the parents are ready to give up and bail out, sympathetic parental support and encouragement is vital. Boundaries should be widened, but they cannot be abandoned. Irresponsible permissiveness on the part of the parents will be interpreted by the adolescent as apathy and a lack of love. Excessive control by the parents will suffocate the normal maturation process that is a part of adolescence. A balanced relationship between parents and adolescents requires parental involvement, mutual respect, and open communication. Such a relationship reduces the chances of loneliness for the adolescent and increases a healthy family atmosphere, the adolescent's "safe haven."

A sense of being rejected by parents or peers also is devastating at this age. Even though adolescents tend to be egocentric, their egos tend to be fragile. Outwardly they may make all sorts of boasts and excuses, displaying an irresponsible invincibility. Within, however, chances are good that they are highly self-critical, possibly seeing themselves as deficient, unattractive, and unacceptable.

Adolescents tend to use "mirror-reflection" self-worth— they see themselves the way they think others are viewing them.

Adolescents tend to use "mirror-reflection" self-worth—they see themselves the way they *think* others are viewing them. A lonely or depressed person will be thinking in negative terms most of the time. Because they think others are thinking negatively of them, they begin to act in ways that reflect their own negative views of themselves. The result is that others will begin to avoid them because of their negative behaviors, thus "proving" that they are deficient, unattractive, and unacceptable to the others.

In one study, Tim Brennan noted a correlation between loneliness and boredom in teens. This may seem like discovering the obvious, but remember what we learned above. Teens are in transition from child to adult. Their childhood roles and behaviors are no longer appropriate, and they have not yet learned their new adult roles with the corresponding appropriate behaviors. At the same time, they want to separate from their parents, who have given them direction and guidance throughout childhood. It's like setting out to sea in a boat without a compass. They may not know how to manage their own time or how to make decisions based on their own likes, dislikes, and values. The result is that in their confusion they tend to do nothing, while at the same time resenting someone telling them what to do. This self-imposed inactivity will lead to social isolation and loneliness.[2]

Brennan also pointed out the confusion of the adolescent's self-image in this time of transition. What is the role of an adolescent in our society? Children are expected to act like children; adults are expected to act like adults. What are adolescents expected to act like? Parents often expect their teenagers to act like adults while they are still treating them like children. The result is role ambiguity. An adolescent, who is thinking, "I don't know who I am, or what others expect of me," may be left feeling alienated and emotionally isolated. Soon he or she concludes, "No one seems to understand me," and worse yet, "No one seems to care."

Feeling respected, accepted, and loved at home
allows adolescents to risk venturing out into their new world,
knowing they have a safety net in case they fall.

Rubenstein and Shaver observed that loneliness tended to be related more to intimacy than to popularity among their teenage subjects. An adolescent with a busy social schedule might still be lonely because personal needs were not being met. However, they noted a gender difference in the same-sex friendship expectations of teens:

> Girls are more anxious than boys about friendship, and their friendships are characterized by more tension, jealousy, and conflict. . . . Boys were generally more relaxed about and distant from their friends. They wanted friends mostly for cooperation, amiability, and assistance in times of trouble. They were less interested than girls in emotional intimacy. . . . Having a positive self-image, for most teen-agers, means having friends and feeling accepted.[3]

It is a natural process of maturation for adolescents to begin to look to their peers more than to their parents for self-image checks. However, like the toddler who played the game, "Mommy, I'm leaving you; don't you leave me," adolescents are also saying to their parents, "Mom and Dad, I'm leaving you, but be there when I need you!" Feeling respected, accepted, and loved at home allows adolescents to risk venturing out into their new world, knowing they have a safety net in case they fall.

Early adulthood

One of the main differences between adolescence and early adulthood is that the longed-for separation from parents actually takes place. Young adults either go off to college, enter the military, get a "real job" and move into their own apartment, or get married. Such changes in lifestyle will result in a time of loneliness for almost everyone. The key factor at this time is how long the experience of loneliness lasts.

In her work with students at UCLA, Carolyn Cutrona found several factors related to lingering loneliness. These included low self-esteem, dissatisfaction with relationships, and lack of social skills. She also noted that both the students who overcame their loneliness and those who lingered in loneliness often tried the same things (such as, becoming involved in school activities, going to parties, improving appearance and social skills, meeting new people). The difference was to be found in their attitudes.[4]

Those who overcame their loneliness were more positive and hopeful about future relationships. Those who remained lonely tended to make excuses, to give up on forming new relationships, and to focus on other aspects of student life. Chronically lonely students put more emphasis on a romantic relationship as the only answer. Finally, they tended to blame themselves for their lingering loneliness.

As one moves into adulthood, there are certain cognitive changes occurring. The individual is more in tune with his or her own desires, needs, and values. There is a trend toward less dependence on the likes and dislikes of others in making decisions. In essence, the young adult becomes more of a thinker.

The source of loneliness for the young adult becomes more one of thoughts and attitudes about self than lack of opportunity or skills for social interaction.

As a result, the source of loneliness for the young adult becomes more one of thoughts and attitudes about self than lack of opportunity or skills for social interaction. Several typical thought patterns develop. The lingering lonely person may be caught in the trap of "either-or" thinking. For example, a young adult thinks, "Either I am involved in a love relationship or I will be lonely for the rest of my life." Another cognitive trap can be that of "I-think-therefore-I-am" thinking. The attitude comes across, "I think I'm worthless, deficient, unlovable; therefore, I am, and no one can ever love me!" Unrealistic expectations of self or others can be just as much of a snare. A lonely young adult thinks, "I should be able to have an intimate relationship with this person," or "It must be my fault!" Deadly comparisons surface with these thoughts, "Look at what Bill and Julie have. If I have anything less than that, it isn't worth having!"

Just because young adults are becoming thinkers does not mean that they automatically become correct thinkers. Perhaps, sometime in the past, they came to believe that they just were not good enough or that *everyone* must like them in order for them to be good, lovable people. They must grow out of such attitudes. Distorted beliefs such as these can be deadly in their efforts to overcome loneliness.

Another possibility for incorrect thinking is not knowing the difference between taking responsibility and blaming. Taking responsibility acknowledges that our thoughts, feelings, opinions, and behaviors are our own and accepts the consequences of them. On the other hand, blaming seeks to attribute absolute causality to someone or something for a situation. Self-blame might attribute one's loneliness to being unlovable, or it might blame others for the isolation. Accepting responsibility, however, might acknowledge that your likes and dislikes make you different from others.

Having self-respect and taking responsibility is healthy and realistic. Blaming is unrealistic and rarely, if ever, has positive results. A healthy self-image in Christ (see chapter 3) is necessary for a positive attitude as a young adult seeking friendships in a new world.

Middle adulthood

Several sources of loneliness in middle adulthood have already been covered elsewhere. Loneliness in marriage and loneliness resulting from divorce or death have been addressed in chapter 5 under those headings. Loneliness as a parent due to "empty nest" syndrome has also been covered in chapter 5. If a middle-aged adult is single, much of what is covered in this chapter under early adulthood may apply.

However, one area is somewhat unique to middle-aged Christians, more so with women than with men. A Christian woman, who may have been previously married and who has children, can feel great loneliness. Unlike young adults who have considerably more "freedom of choice" in establishing a new intimate relationship, these women are limited by the number of available Christian men of similar age. There may also be hesitancy on the part of potential partners to become involved with a "ready-made" family. Christian women of middle adulthood who have always been single also have the same restriction regarding the availability of single Christian men of similar age. In addition, a middle-aged Christian may have a sense of time running out for a new meaningful relationship.

A Christian man or woman who has already had an intimate, affectionate, and sexual relationship with a spouse knows what is missing and misses it all the more.

A Christian man or woman who has already had an intimate, affectionate, and sexual relationship with a spouse knows what is missing and misses it all the more. God created our bodies according to his divine plan, and this includes our sexuality. Even though the affectionate and sexual partner may now be gone, the needs and desires for affection and sex are still present. Single Christians in this age group, who have never been married, may fear that they will never be able to experience the intimacy, affection, and sexual fulfillment of marriage.

Unbelieving friends might suggest that there is no problem; if you want sex, go out and get it wherever you can. God has a different plan. Scripture reminds us that sexual activity is a blessing within marriage but a sin outside of marriage. Because of this, there may be a strong temptation to enter immediately into another intimate relationship that offers the probability of marriage, especially if there is an eligible potential partner of similar age. We want so much to have what we once had and enjoyed, or never yet had, that we are ready to enter a relationship to overcome our loneliness.

We are going after the right thing, but we are doing it the wrong way. Do not rush into any such relationship. Take time to follow these steps:

- Decide what you want in a partner. Think about your past marriage or the marriages of others. What do you want to keep? What do you want to change? (See chapter 5.)

- Learn to live alone before you seek a permanent relationship; get to know yourself better. (See chapter 7.)

- Develop friendships rather than intimate relationships. The only thing a friend cannot give you that marriage can is sex. (See chapter 8.) Healthy intimate relationships develop from good friendships.

- If the need or desire for sex is strong, give this battle between what is natural and what is temptation to the Lord. Ask for God's power. Most cannot be content and single without a special gift from God. In his time, God will provide an appropriate partner or the ability to remain single without a sense of loneliness. Continue to live a chaste and decent life; it's the Lord's will.

- Put your trust in the Lord. Wait for his time schedule to take effect; don't try to force him into yours.

Late Adulthood

Too many myths equate old age with loneliness. Research has shown repeatedly that, overall, older adults are often the least lonely age group. As always, this depends on the individual's circumstances. The most frequently cited factors related to loneliness among the elderly have to do with some form of loss, such as, the loss of a loved one or friend, loss of health, loss of income, loss of independence, or loss of perceived social role.[5]

Many have studied the social interaction of older adults with family, friends, and neighbors and its relation to loneliness. No clear answer emerges to questions like, "How much interaction is necessary to avoid loneliness?" or "What kind of interaction is best?"

Gary Lee and Masako Ishii-Kuntz made some interesting observations based on their studies. The research indicated that the factor that influenced a sense of well-being most was mutual consent. The well-being or loneliness of an elderly person was less dependent on the amount of social interaction or whether it was with family or friends. Instead loneliness diminished if both parties wanted to be together. If the elderly person felt a sense of obligation to be with family, either siblings or adult children, the interaction was not highly correlated with a sense of well-being. On the other hand, if the elderly person was involved in an activity with either a family member or a friend by mutual choice, this had a positive influence on his or her sense of well-being. For older adults, the quality and meaning of the interaction with another influenced the level of an individual's sense of well-being or loneliness.[6]

For older adults, the quality and meaning
of the interaction with another influenced the level
of an individual's sense of well-being or loneliness.

Living alone does not necessarily make the elderly person lonely. Some people choose to be alone a good share of the time because they enjoy the solitude and find personal fulfillment in solitary activities. Loneliness is more likely to be a problem if living alone is not by choice. Mobility may be one factor that plays into the acceptability of living alone. If the older adult is able to drive or has easy access to transportation, living alone does not necessarily mean being socially isolated. The warning signs of loneliness for someone living alone are depression and social withdrawal.

For almost any older adult, a time of loneliness intrudes when a loved one dies. A reasonable time for grieving is one to two years. The intensity and duration of bereavement depends on the level of intimacy that was within the relationship. Research has found, however, that dealing with widowhood may be easier in old age than at an earlier age because there is an expectation that loved ones and friends will be dying. In addition, it appears that widowhood tends to be harder on older men than on older women. One thought is that husbands often, though not always, rely more on their wives for daily care and needs.[7]

Most retired people are happy and satisfied with the opportunity to spend more time together or alone doing the things they enjoy doing.

Retirement does not automatically usher in a period of prolonged loneliness for older adults. A period of adjustment to the change in social roles and activities may include a brief period of situational loneliness. The fact is, most retired people are happy and satisfied with the opportunity to spend more time together or alone doing the things they enjoy doing. If the retirement is involuntary, forced because of poor health, or results in a significantly lower financial standard of living, then depression and loneliness may occur. Once again, the individual circumstances contribute to loneliness more than the retirement itself.

Poor health and poor financial status may lead to social isolation or reduced social activity for an older adult or couple. Interestingly, a person's perception of these potential problems influences their sense of loneliness. For example, if the person or couple does not perceive that their situation is detrimental, that their circumstances are beyond their control, or that their situation was forced upon them, then loneliness is less likely to occur. Jeff Young observed that if a person's internal reality, that is, a person's expectations of a situation, corresponded with the external reality of the situation, then less anxiety, depression, and loneliness occurred.[8]

Being old and being lonely are not inevitable twins.

Being old and being lonely are not inevitable twins. An older adult's level of loneliness depends on the circumstances and the individual's perception of the situation. In addition, being alone does not automatically result in loneliness for the older adult any more than being with someone automatically means happiness, satisfaction, and fulfillment. Times of loss and changes in life will result in a period of grieving and loneliness for most people—young and old alike. If the sense of loneliness is prolonged or becomes chronic (lasting more than two years), then the individual and family should be concerned and begin looking for help.

Summary

Loneliness is a universal human experience. In general, the time of greatest vulnerability to loneliness is adolescence. The significant number of changes a teenager experiences contributes to the problem. Younger children can also experience loneliness. Parents play an important role in the loneliness of their children. It is not that parents "make" their children lonely, but that through an understanding of a child's worldview and open communication, parents can reduce the impact of loneliness on their children.

People with a healthy, positive self-esteem tend to be less lonely than those with a poor self-image. Appreciation of self allows a person to be alone and to enjoy solitude. Additionally, people with positive attitudes tend to be more attractive to others than those with negative self-views. Parents can help their children achieve a positive self-image through support, mutual respect, and personal involvement in their children's lives. This will carry over into adolescence and adulthood as well.

At any age, the experience of loss is correlated with loneliness. The intensity of the loneliness will depend on the level of intimacy in the relationship or on the personal meaning attached to an inanimate object or place. Although older adults may experience more losses than younger people, they are often better able to work through the grieving process, thus reducing the impact of their loneliness.

At one time or another, everybody will experience loneliness.

At one time or another, everybody will experience loneliness. For some it will be situational; for others it will be a lingering loneliness. Perhaps a change in the circumstances of the situation will reduce the loneliness. Most often, however, a change is needed in the person's attitude, self-image, or world-view in order to alleviate the loneliness. At any age, one needs to learn how to live as a child of God, how to be a friend, and how to depend on the most faithful Friend, Jesus Christ, in order to end the loneliness.

NOTES

[1]John Killinger, *The Loneliness of Children*, (New York: Vanguard Press, 1980), pp. 8,10.

[2]Tim Brennan, "Loneliness at Adolescence," in *Loneliness: A Source Book of Current Theory, Research and Therapy*, edited by Letitia A. Peplau and Daniel Perlman, (New York: John Wiley & Sons, 1982), pp. 269-290.

[3]Carin Rubenstein and Phillip Shaver, *In Search of Intimacy*, (New York: Delacorte Press, 1982), pp. 77,78.

[4]Carolyn Cutrona, "Transition to College: Loneliness and the Process of Social Adjustment," in *Loneliness: A Source Book of Current Theory, Research and Therapy*, edited by Letitia A. Peplau and Daniel Perlman, (New York: John Wiley & Sons, 1982), pp. 291-309.

[5]Rubenstein and Shaver.

[6]Gary Lee and Masako Ishii-Kuntz, "Social Interaction, Loneliness, and Emotional Well-being among the Elderly," *Research on Aging*, Vol. 9, No. 4, 1987, pp. 459-482.

[7]Rubenstein and Shaver.

[8]Jeff Young, "Loneliness, Depression, and Cognitive Therapy: Theory and Application." in *Loneliness: A Source Book of Current Theory, Research and Therapy*, edited by Letitia A. Peplau and Daniel Perlman, (New York: John Wiley & Sons, 1982), pp. 379-405.

CHAPTER 7:

Learning to Live with Myself

Introduction

We've talked enough about loneliness; now let's do something about it! As paradoxical as it may seem, the first step in overcoming loneliness—not just coping with it—is learning how to be alone. If we learn how to live with ourselves, we begin to learn how to live with others. This requires three elements:

- a proper understanding of God's relationship with us (see chapter 2),
- a healthy self-image as a child of God (see chapter 3), and
- an honest identity of myself as an individual.

You may wish to review chapters 2 and 3, after you finish this chapter.

The first step in overcoming loneliness—

not just coping with it—

is learning how to be alone.

A proper understanding of God's relationship with us

Because of our sins, God should abandon us. That is what we deserve from him. God, however, did the unexpected and loved us in spite of our sins. Paul reminds us, "God demonstrates his own love for us in this: While we were still sinners, Christ died for us" (Romans 5:8). Remember that Jesus cried from the cross, "My God, my God, why have you forsaken me?" (Matthew 27:46). Jesus was forsaken so that we would never be forsaken. He removed our sins by his suffering and death on the cross. Because of what Jesus accomplished, we enter a new relationship with God. We are his children. This thought bears repeating because our sinful nature works hard to cause us to forget the undeserved love of God for us.

Jesus was forsaken so that we would never be forsaken.

As his children, God has promised us, "'Never will I leave you; never will I forsake you.' So we say with confidence, 'The Lord is my helper; I will not be afraid'" (Hebrews 13:5,6). With the apostle Paul we are also able to confidently say,

> We know that in all things God works for the good of those who love him, who have been called according to his purpose. . . . What, then, shall we say in response to this? If God is for us, who can be against us? He who did not spare his own Son, but gave him up for us all—how will he not also, along with him, graciously give us all things? . . . Who shall separate us from the love of Christ? Shall trouble or hardship or persecution or famine or nakedness or danger or sword? . . . No, in all these things we are more than conquerors through him who loved us. For I am convinced that neither death nor life, neither angels nor demons, neither the present nor the future, nor any powers, neither height nor depth, nor anything else in all creation, will be able to separate us from the love of God that is in Christ Jesus our Lord." (Romans 8:28-39)

We have a heavenly Father who loves us, understands us, and promises never to leave us to face this world alone. Our sinful nature seeks to make us believe that God does not care anymore, that we are so worthless that not even God can love us anymore, or that nobody else cares about us. But the truth is much different. Imagine that God is on the other side of a two-way mirror. He is right here—only six inches away—but when we look for him, we see only a reflection of how we see ourselves. We feel abandoned by God because we see things from our own perspective and fail to recall his love and promises.

What we think we are seeing in our life may not be full reality. Often we think because we feel worthless, forsaken, and forgotten, that we actually are. Such reasoning comes from our sinful nature. Rather, as children of God through faith in Jesus, we need to let the Holy Spirit use God's Word to change our way of thinking and feeling. By faith we know we are loved by God, even if at times we do not perceive any evidence of it in our lives.

As Christians, we understand what Paul wrote, "We live by faith, not by sight" (2 Corinthians 5:7). We do not live by feelings. We are loved by God, and we have an eternal home waiting for us after this life is over. In faith we are also assured that we have God with us here, right now. He has us cradled in his loving arms as our Good Shepherd. We may FEEL totally abandoned, neglected, and isolated. We are NOT.

By faith we know we are loved by God,

even if at times we do not perceive any evidence of it

in our lives.

Look over the passages of comfort and encouragement at the end of chapter 2. Pick several of them that have personal meaning for you. Write them down on an index card; carry them with you in your pocket or purse; memorize them; read them daily and consider their message for you personally. Whenever you are in the "stinking thinking" of loneliness, let the Holy Spirit renew your faith and confidence in the Lord through those promises. The Holy Spirit comes to you in the words of the gospel whenever you use them, wherever you are.

It is also important to renew your prayer relationship with God. Turn your worries, anxieties, and blues into conversations with God. For instance, when you think, "O great, another day all by myself with nobody to talk to or do anything with." Turn this self-defeating thought into a prayer. Simply pray, "Dear heavenly Father, I am alone today. Be with me and open my mind and heart to your loving presence. Help we to realize that you are always listening to my prayers even when no one else is here. Amen." When we turn our worries into prayers, we may still have some of the same questions, but at least we are going to the right One for the answers. When our sinful nature tempts us to believe that our prayers are just bouncing off the ceiling, we need to dispute that lie with the truth of God's Word. Our heavenly Father is with us; he hears us; he answers our every prayer; we are never alone.

- Call upon me in the day of trouble; I will deliver you, and you will honor me. (Psalm 50:15)
- Listen to my prayer, O God, do not ignore my plea; hear me and answer me. My thoughts trouble me and I am distraught . . . My heart is in anguish within me; . . . But I call to God, and the LORD saves me. Evening, morning and noon I cry out in distress, and he hears my voice. . . . Cast your cares on the LORD and he will sustain you. (Psalm 55)
- Yet I am always with you; you hold me by my right hand. You guide me with your counsel, and afterward you will take me into glory. (Psalm 73:23,24)

Healthy self-image as a child of God

Each one of us is a uniquely created and eternally redeemed child of God in Christ. No two people on this earth have the same combination of gifts, faith, developed personality, and life experiences. It is for this reason that making comparisons with another person is invalid and often dangerous. Comparisons that leave us on the short end are especially deadly to our self-image. Thus God tells us in Galatians 6:4,5: "Each one should test his own actions. Then he can take pride in himself, without comparing himself to somebody else, for each one should carry his own load."

No two people on this earth have the same combination
of gifts, faith, developed personality, and life experiences.

As a child of God, each one is a member of the body of Christ. Let's review the lessons of chapter 3 and consider what it means to be a part of the body of Christ. If God made you to be a foot, he has given you the gifts necessary to be a foot. You can run, walk, balance, and sift sand through your toes. But God has also given you some inabilities. For example, as a foot, you cannot hold a glass of water, screw a light bulb into the ceiling light fixture, or digest food. As a part of the body of Christ, you do not have to be able to do everything others can do. That is the reason God made hands, stomachs, and so forth. Of course, you are not a foot. You are a human being and a child of God. Yet you have a unique collection of gifts that no one else has.

When you are doing the best you can each day
with what God gives you for that day,
you can feel good about yourself.
Your daily sins are washed away in Christ
so that you can use your abilities, your inabilities, and
your current circumstances as a child of God.

Does that make sense to you? You are who God made you to be as his child in Christ. To try to be someone or something else is self-defeating. When you are doing the best you can each day with what God gives you for that day, you can feel good about yourself. Your daily sins are washed away in Christ so that you can use your abilities, your inabilities, and your current circumstances as a child of God. The result is a healthy self-image in Christ. You are a forgiven child of God, able to serve God and others with the gifts God has given you.

Unrealistic expectations are just as unhealthy as deadly comparisons. Unrealistic expectations develop when we accept someone else's standards as our own without first testing their validity for us. These standards can either be set too high or too low, although most often they are set too high. Unfortunately we sometimes measure our worth on the basis of those standards. For example, an adolescent who weighs 130 pounds expects to play college football because his friend's brother plays. His friend's brother, however, weighs 240 and comes from an athletic family. Such unrealistic expectations may lead us to think we are worthless, helpless, and hopeless. After a series of perceived failures, we see ourselves as unable to do a thing. Then we give up trying to do anything. The truth is that we set an expectation or standard that was higher than our God-given abilities, inabilities, and circumstances. Perhaps we set the expectation ourselves, or maybe someone else set it for us. Instead of testing our actions and worth based on God's grace and mercy, we swallow the unrealistic expectation as our only standard of measurement, thus thinking more highly of ourselves than we should.

We are unwise when we use our own standards for testing our worth and developing a self-image, because we tend to use shoulds *and* musts: . . . *The problem with* shoulds *and* musts *is that often they are not based on the reality of our God-given abilities.*

We are unwise when we use our own standards for testing our worth and developing a self-image, because we tend to use *shoulds* and *musts*: "I should be able to do better;" or "I must get an A or I'm a failure!" The problem with *shoulds* and *musts* is that often they are not based on the reality of our God-given abilities, inabilities, and current circumstances. For example, just because a student gets A's in English, history, and Spanish, the parents may assume that their child should also get A's in algebra and biology as well. Reality says God may have given the student the ability to achieve *C*'s in math and science. However, the student internalizes the parents' *should*; and every time he scores a *C*, the result is a sense of failure, even though the student is working to the best of his God-given ability.

Eventually, continual "failures" result in a deterioration of self-worth and self-image that begins with disappointment, grows into discouragement, then into depression, and may even end finally with despair. The key factor in this loss of self-image and lowering of self-esteem is that the person has set an unrealistic expectation. When we do get *A*'s, our boast can rightly be "Way to go; I did a good job! Thank you, God, for giving me the ability!" And when we do our best and get a lower grade, we can also say, "Way to go, I did the best I could! Thank you, God, for your gifts to me."

In view of God's mercy, take an honest inventory of your abilities, inabilities, and current circumstances. If you see yourself only in negative terms, do not rely on your own judgment. Ask others who know you to tell you what they see as your abilities. If someone says, "You're a good student," or "You're a good mother," remember that these represent a broad set of abilities. What are the specific tasks and duties involved in being a student or a mother? Each one of those tasks and duties requires an ability, a talent, a skill. If you look at those specific tasks and abilities required of a student or mother, you will be surprised how your inventory will grow in length. God has given you the ability to do many things.

By refuting our deadly comparisons and
unrealistic expectations,
along with any other negative self-talk,
we are in a better position
to look at ourselves in sober judgment.

The next step is to listen to any negative self-talk. What do you say to yourself when you make a mistake? If you are really down on yourself, perhaps this is the place to start. What *shoulds* and *musts* are driving your actions and your measurements of those actions? When you have discovered them, refute them with positive, realistic statements. For instance, if every time I make a mistake, I think, "You idiot! How could you do that?" my realistic refutation might be, "Wait a minute; it's only a mistake. I know I am forgiven in Christ. The world didn't end. What do I need to do now? Ask for help?" That, of course, might trigger a *must* or *should* response: "You should be able to do it yourself," "If I'm worth anything at all, I must figure it out myself," or "To ask for help is a sign of weakness and failure. I must do it myself." Part of being a member of the body of Christ is accepting our own inabilities and weaknesses. This gives us permission to ask other members of the body for help because God wants the body to work together to his glory. Our real strength is in the Lord, not in ourselves.

By refuting our deadly comparisons and unrealistic expectations, along with any other negative self-talk, we are in a better position to look at ourselves in sober judgment. Coupled with our honest inventory of our gifts and circumstances, we now have a valid standard by which to measure our worth and develop a self-image in view of God's mercy and grace in Christ.

Identifying myself as an individual

This last element of learning to live with oneself builds on the first two. First of all, let us make a distinction between being an individual and being independent. Webster's *New World Dictionary* defines *independent* as "free from the influence or control of others; self determined, self-reliant." The same dictionary defines *individuality* as "the sum of the characteristics that set one person or thing apart."

Identifying yourself as an individual acknowledges that you are a unique creation of God

Identifying yourself as an individual acknowledges that you are a unique creation of God. It also allows you to "[belong] to all the others" (Romans 12:5). Being an individual allows a person to be *interdependent* with others. Because each of us is a unique creation of God, each one has something to offer to the others in his or her various relationships. When we appreciate our own individuality, we are able to appreciate the individuality of others as well. From a personal perspective, they have something to offer me, and I have something to offer them. Our relationship, then, is one of reciprocity which can be summarized as a give/give, receive/receive relationship, in which all persons are valued and appreciated. This is in keeping with God's plan for the members of the body of Christ. God does not desire us to be self-reliant or free from the influence of others. Instead Jesus draws us together into his body through faith.

Mutual respect is an important element of true friendship.
It becomes a source of trust and intimacy
between two individuals.

When I respect myself as an individual child of God in view of God's mercy and grace in Christ, I am better able to respect others in my life. This mutual respect is an important element of true friendship. It becomes a source of trust and intimacy between two individuals. The result is a growing together into a "we-ness" relationship, without forfeiting each one's individuality. In this way we have "equal concern for each other" (1 Corinthians 12:25) as God desires, and we can help "carry each other's burdens" (Galatians 6:2) without fear of becoming a burden to one another.

Being alone

A relationship with God based on his grace and mercy results in two important advantages to combat loneliness:

- a healthy self-image as a child of God in Christ and
- an identity of yourself as an individual with something to offer others in a relationship.

These advantages allow a Christian to be comfortable with himself or herself. In this comfort zone, Christians are able to be by themselves and enjoy it without fear of being lonely. We know what we can do and not do, and we can enjoy doing what we do. We do not need the approval of others because all we do, we do as "living sacrifices, holy and pleasing to God" (Romans 12:1).

There are times, as an individual child of God, when each of us will want to be alone. Perhaps we will even want to experience some solitude in order to get "close to God." We are comfortable in doing this, once again, because we do not need the approval of others, nor are we dependent on others for our thoughts and feelings. Feeling good about oneself as an individual child of God in Christ is God's plan for each one of us. It is our sinful nature that seeks to destroy our image of ourselves and then our relationship with God through self-defeating thoughts, feelings, and behaviors.

> *As we come to like ourselves as redeemed individuals,*
> *we will become more comfortable around others,*
> *and others will like us as well,*
> *as we share common interests and experiences.*

By the grace of God and the power of the Holy Spirit in his Word, we can defeat our sinful nature, refute all that is self-defeating, and learn to love and even like ourselves in Christ. The Holy Spirit then gives us the power to pray. For Christians, prayer becomes an important part of our efforts to develop our individuality. We can come to God in prayer, asking for his help. He patiently listens to us, to all our troubles and worries, and then responds to our requests in a way that is ultimately best for us and for other believers. Because of God's love for us in Christ and the power of the Holy Spirit through the Word, an amazing thing can take place. As we come to like ourselves as redeemed individuals, we will become more comfortable around others, and others will like us as well, as we share common interests and experiences. That is what we call friendship.

ADDITIONAL READING

Recommended reading from the secular press that expands on what is presented in this chapter includes:

1. David Burns, *Feeling Good: The New Mood Therapy*, (New York: Signet, 1980).
2. Albert Ellis, *A New Guide to Rational Living*, (N. Hollywood, CA: Wilshire, 1975).

Remember to use the filter of God's Word when reading these or any books. They offer helpful information, but not everything they contain agrees with God's Word.

CHAPTER 8:

Learning to Be a Friend

Introduction

In the previous chapter we learned how to live with ourselves—the basics of a healthy self-image and self-esteem as children of God in Christ. Romans 12 tells us that we are to "belong to all the others" as members of the body of Christ. The emphasis is on our activity of belonging to others, rather than on our waiting to find someone to "belong" to us. The purpose of this final chapter is to help us learn how to be a friend and be prepared for that intimate relationship we may be seeking.

Jesus Christ: the always true friend

In their book *Friend of the Lonely Heart*, Josh McDowell and Norm Wakefield identified four types of unhealthy friendships that might lead to loneliness.

1. Part-time friends—with you only when they have no one else to be with
2. Conditional friends—your friends, IF you do what they want
3. Undependable friends—only think of themselves and not about you
4. Superficial friends—act more like mere acquaintances rather than someone who really cares[1]

Yet even when all these other "friends" fail us, we still have one true Friend—Jesus Christ. He is a full-time Friend, who has promised never to leave us nor forsake us. His friendship is unconditional, built on grace and forgiveness. He is always dependable. He will always be there for us, not just when we think we need him, but all the time. Finally, his friendship with us is meaningful—he cares about us and wants to listen to our every thought, feeling, need, desire, complaint, and joy. Jesus is the true, best Friend from whom we can learn much about being a friend to others.

If we were to sum up all of the characteristics of Jesus' friendship with us, we might say that Jesus has a deep interest in others. Think about it. Jesus definitely doesn't just think about himself and what he can get out of our relationship. He harbors no ego interested only in its own likes, needs, and wants. The cross of Calvary proved that. Nor is he just a "yes-person," who gives in to whatever we want, letting us always have our way just to keep us as a friend. He cares enough about our relationship to speak up when we are headed in the wrong direction and lead us back onto the right path. Jesus is always there for us. He is always thinking what is best for our relationship. He wants us to be friends forever.

The fear of friendship

To be a friend requires what we call "we-ness" thinking. To have a lasting friendship requires mutual "we-ness" thinking. I can be a friend to someone, but if there is no reciprocal response from the other person, a true friendship cannot grow. The fear of being rejected, abandoned, or ignored by the person with whom we want to be close may keep us from even approaching that person. It is like we are already saying no for them to any relationship with them. That fear actually comes from "I-ness" thinking, which says, "I don't want to get hurt, so I will do nothing." Sure, such thinking keeps us safe from the risk of rejection, but we will still feel lonely and rejected.

*The process of overcoming the fear of rejection and
its tendency towards passivity begins within oneself.*

This fear of rejection and abandonment can easily lead a lonely person into a state of passivity. In that state, the person either does nothing or waits for someone to do something. The process of overcoming the fear of rejection and its tendency towards passivity begins within oneself. Chapters 3 and 7 explain the traps of poor self-image and low self-esteem and how to overcome them in view of God's mercy in Christ. If you have not read these chapters as yet, please do so before continuing any further into this chapter. None of what is suggested in this chapter will happen if you still see yourself as worthless, helpless, hopeless, and unlovable.

Feeling good—looking good

God tells us in 1 Peter 3:3,4: "Your beauty should not come from outward adornment, such as braided hair and the wearing of gold jewelry and fine clothes. Instead, it should be that of your inner self, the unfading beauty of a gentle and quiet spirit, which is of great worth in God's sight." The Lord is not telling us that he does not want us to dress nicely or take care of our physical appearance. On the other hand, he *is* telling us a very important truth—true, lasting beauty comes from within. People do not need to look like superstar models, movies stars, or athletes in order to be attractive to others. We just need to be ourselves—provided we feel good about ourselves.

True, lasting beauty comes from within.

Picture two people coming into a room. One is stooped-shouldered, wearing a plain, drab, saggy suit. Mousy hair hangs in her face. She has downcast eyes and a frown, and she shuffles along the wall and around the outer edge of the crowd. The other person walks in with straight posture, shoulders back; wearing a fitted suit which is neither new nor stylish, it just looks good on her. Her hair is styled to fit the contours of her face. She has a bright smile and makes momentary eye contact with a slight nod of the head to others. With a steady pace she approaches the crowd. The person could just as well be a man as a woman. Which of the two people are you interested in meeting? The fact is, they are the same person. Which do you think came first—a change in hair and dress style or a change in self-perception? Studies show that people who begin to feel good about themselves tend to take better care of their physical appearance. The change in self-perception came first.[2]

Because first impressions count when meeting others . . .
Nonverbal communication, or body language,
plays an important part in creating good first impressions.

Because first impressions count when meeting others, what can we do to improve our chances of becoming a friend with someone? Nonverbal communication, or body language, plays an important part in creating good first impressions. Here are some things you can do to improve those messages you transmit to others when you first meet them.

- *Facial expression:* Practice smiling in a mirror. Become aware of what the muscles in your face feel like when you have a smile that shows your teeth with slightly parted lips and upturned corners of your mouth. Relax the muscles in your forehead, so that the furrows smooth out. Look yourself straight in the eyes. Without staring, periodically shift your focus from one eye of your reflection to the other and blink every once in a while. After you have practiced this enough to be comfortable with it, walk down the street (unless the local culture or neighborhood pose a threat to your personal safety) and smile at individuals as they approach you. If they do not smile back, it does not matter because you do not know them anyway, so it is nothing personal about you or them. If they do smile back, it means you may have put a little sunshine into their day.
- *Posture:* Practice standing sideways in front of a mirror with your shoulders slightly back, back straight, and head erect. When

you are comfortable with how this feels, walk around the room in this posture. Let your arms swing gently back and forth at your side as you walk. Walk with a casual but firm step—this is not a march. Now practice standing and walking while holding a plate or glass, as if you are at a party, until you feel comfortable with the posture. Finally, practice both your posture and your facial expressions in front of the mirror until you are comfortable with them.

- *Physical appearance:* More than anything else in body language, physical appearance is a matter of personal taste. If you can afford it, get your hair done professionally in a style that compliments your facial contours and body shape. Use make-up to highlight your face, not to remake it. If it needs to be said, shower or bathe daily and use deodorant. Go to the dentist and have your teeth cleaned; then brush, floss, and rinse regularly. Perfume, cologne, or aftershave are optional accents to your appearance. When it comes to your clothing, remember that you do not need to wear the most fashionable clothing. Just wear something that looks good on you and fits well. Choose a style and color that does not just draw attention to the clothes themselves. Remember that looking attractive does not require that you look "sexy." Let your clothing express that you feel good about yourself.

Feeling good—and saying so

The next concern in learning to be a friend is acquiring some basic communication skills. You have walked into a room and made a good impression with your facial expression, posture, and physical appearance. Now it is time to start a conversation with someone. Here are a few hints on what to do next.

- *Eye contact:* In American culture, maintaining eye contact is considered a way of showing respect to the person with whom you are speaking. Just do what you practiced in the mirror, and you will do fine in this skill. Whether speaking or listening, maintain comfortable eye contact without staring.
- *Proximity and touching:* Keep in mind that in American culture, people tend to have a "bubble" of personal space that they protect as their own. This circle of approximately 18 inches in radius is their "intimate zone." Do not enter it unless you are invited. A safe distance to stand from a person in a casual conversation is about two feet; unless, of course, the room is crowded. Touching has become a "touchy" subject in our country, due to a fear of it being mistaken for sexual harassment,

molestation, or assault. It is safest not to initiate any touching other than a handshake, which is acceptable for both genders. Perhaps, however, the situation calls for touching (as when giving comfort to someone who is grieving). To be safe in such cases, let your hand rest momentarily and lightly on the person's hand, arm, or shoulder. These are generally considered to be safe-touch zones.

- *Speech patterns:* The apostle Peter tells us to speak "with gentleness and respect" (1 Peter 3:15) when speaking of our faith. This is a good pattern to follow at all times. Speaking loudly and boisterously tends to turn people off. Speaking too softly forces them to try harder to listen than they may deem worthwhile for casual conversation. Speak gently, but with enough volume to be heard by those in your circle of conversation. A rapid, pressured pace of speaking is often difficult to listen to over a period of time. It tends to result in others becoming nervous and uneasy. If you are a rapid speaker, practice speaking more slowly into a tape recorder until you are comfortable with it. If you tend to speak so slowly that others appear to get antsy waiting for you to complete a thought, then practice speaking at a little faster pace. A way to figure out a good pace is to listen to others talking in casual conversations and adjust accordingly.

- *Listening and attending:* It is important that the other person has a sense that you are listening. There are a few basic techniques that you can use to send this message of interest and attention.

  a) *Face the person squarely.* Either turn your whole body, if possible, or turn your face toward the person while she is talking.

  b) *Lean toward the person.* This can be merely a slight incline of the head toward the person while he is talking, or it can be a general movement of the body toward the person if the situation requires it.

  c) *Be open in posture.* If sitting, do not cross your legs toward the person; if standing, do not tightly cross your arms against your chest. Both of these closed postures can give a message of discomfort with, or pushing away from, the person.

  d) *Maintain eye contact.* Again, in American culture this is an important sign of respect and caring.

  e) *Be relaxed.* At least look like you want to be there talking with the person by striking a casual pose without the appearance of rigid muscle tension.

Thus far we have talked about how to look and what to do when initiating contact with another person in conversation.

The next question is the big one: what to say. There are four areas to consider when thinking about what to say—surface or small talk, questions about the other person, self-disclosure, and empathic statements.[3]

- **Surface or small talk:** David Burns suggests that before going to a party or meeting with someone, take time to look through the newspaper or a news magazine to be aware of current events. Cover several areas of interest, such as, local and world news, business, arts, and sports, so that you are equipped to establish a common ground of conversation with the other person. Surface talk explores noncontroversial things and events. It is a "safe zone" in conversation because you are not talking about anything personal. In meeting a new person, stay in the "safe zone" for a while until there is a mutual desire to move into a deeper conversation.

- **Questions:** The person who asks the questions controls the topic of conversation. If you are seeking information from a person, and you ask a lot of questions, you will get only the information you request. That is the downside to asking questions. On the positive side, many people enjoy talking about themselves; therefore you will appear to be an interesting conversationalist if you continue to ask open-ended questions that allow them to do so. An open-ended question is one that begins with "who, what, where, when, how, or why." This requires at least a sentence in reply. Any question that begins with a verb can be answered with merely a yes or no, and the conversation stops. Such questions are called closed-ended questions and should be avoided. Notice the difference between these two questions and answers.

Closed-ended question

"Do you like the new _____ ?" The person can answer yes or no and say nothing more. The conversation also comes to a stop until someone goes on with a new idea or a new question. This question does not involve the person giving the answer.

Open-ended question

"What do you think about the new _____ ?" The response to this question must be more than just a yes or no. The person will answer with an opinion, and the conversation has a chance to grow and continue.

Keep in mind that when you ask for an opinion, you may get the answer you are not expecting, and you may disagree with the answer. Sometimes expressing deeply held opinions may scare others away. Surface talk is not meant to lead into arguments. Take a moment to think before responding, and find some way to give a neutral response. Then you can either give your own opinion or change the subject.

Neutral response

If the person answers your question, "I don't like it. I don't see any value in it," you might reply, "I've heard that opinion from others. That's a possibility." Then you can stop, change the subject or give your opinion in a God-pleasing way rather than reacting with a strong comment, such as, "How can you think that way? It's a wonderful _____ !" Consider what you may want to say and how you want to say it based on the following discussion about self-disclosure.

There is often a danger in revealing too much, too soon.

- **Self-disclosure:** Scaring others away is a hazard of self-disclosure. It is difficult to know how much self-disclosure is useful in a conversation. There is often a danger in revealing too much, too soon. Sometimes when we are lonely and get into a conversation with someone, we want that person to get to know us so much that we start telling them "everything" about us. Most people are not ready for that amount of personal information during initial contacts. On the other hand, if after we have come to know someone a little better and that person continues to say little of a personal nature, we may begin to wonder if we are in a one-sided relationship.

  The key factor in knowing the right amount of self-disclosure is reciprocity. Are both of you sharing your own feelings, thoughts, opinions, needs, and desires with one another about a subject or mutual interest? Is it all coming from you? Is one person self-disclosing about only one area of interest, such as hobbies, while the other is "dumping" everything—from occupation, religion, politics, and hobbies to health history, family background, and past relationships? Such a discrepancy in the amount of self-disclosure tends to scare others away.

  One way to understand how much to share with another is the trust/vulnerability balance. We become vulnerable when we tell another person about ourselves. The more we tell a person about ourselves, the more information that person has with which to hurt us. The amount of information that we share about ourselves with someone else is an indicator of our level of trust in that person. If he or she chooses to keep the relationship at a surface level, or if he or she chooses to share our personal information indiscriminately with others, we are vulnerable to feeling abandoned, rejected, or betrayed by that person. As you learn to trust another person, you can disclose more and more of yourself. But we do not share everything about ourselves with everyone. We also become vulnerable when the other person is not investing as much of himself or herself into the relationship as we are. Friendships develop in the balance of trust and vulnerability. Increased mutual trust is a sign of growing intimacy in a relationship.

> *Increased mutual trust is a sign of growing intimacy in a relationship.*

* **Empathic statements:** Empathy is different than sympathy. Sympathy implies taking sides or having a sense of pity for a person. Empathy is a desire to understand a person from that person's perspective, rather than just our own perspective. If we have empathy, we want to see the world through that person's eyes and understand the problems, troubles, and joys of another. Empathic statements are guesses on our part as to the meaning of what a person has just said. Before we respond with our own thoughts or feelings, we want to make sure we really heard what that person was saying to us.

There is a basic empathy formula that goes like this:

"You feel *[state the emotion you think the person is expressing]* because *[state what you guess is the source of that feeling]*."

These empathic guesses need to be stated in your own words but based on what the person was saying. For instance, the person says, "I had a lousy day today," and you respond, "You had a lousy day today." This is only repeating the words, nothing more. At this point it is not an empathic guess. We must go one more step. An empathic statement might be, "You feel rotten because you had a rough time at work today." The person to whom we are talking will appreciate our effort to understand and will either confirm or clarify what we have guessed. This often leads to a deeper level of communication with greater mutual self-disclosure.

Summary

These are a few of the tools necessary for carrying on a conversation. The most important factor, however, is not a tool; it is an attitude. A true friend cares about the other person. A true friend is not so much interested in "What can I get out of this relationship?" but rather "How can I help our relationship to grow?" God tells us in Ephesians 4:29, "Do not let any unwholesome talk come out of your mouths, but only what is helpful for building others up according to their needs, that it may benefit those who listen." Notice the words, "building others up according to their needs."

Using empathic statements without truly caring about the other person will soon be recognized as being hollow and shallow, even hypocritical. Learning to be a friend means learning to think "WE," rather than just "Me" or "Me and You." It is a matter of mutual respect and reciprocity or, as God says in 1 Corinthians 12:25, having "equal concern for each other." We do not use friendship just to satisfy our own needs, nor do we let others use or abuse our friendship.

You will have noticed that this chapter was not about how to build an intimate relationship. That is not our goal. Intimacy between two people develops over time. There first needs to be friendship. Friends provide one another with companionship, love, and concern. Friends will sometimes offer "a shoulder to cry on" and will share mutual interests and activities. These things build mutual respect and, together with a healthy self-image in Christ, are most often what we need to overcome our sense of loneliness. Then intimacy has an opportunity to grow with the friends of our choice.

NOTES

[1]Josh McDowell and Norm Wakefield, *Friend of the Lonely Heart*, (Dallas: Word, 1991), pp. 97-103.

[2]David Burns, *Intimate Connections*, (New York: William Morrow, 1985).

[3]Burns.

David Burns has many good ideas related to learning to live with yourself and becoming a friend. Although we cannot agree with everything he writes (such as, sexual relationships outside of marriage), he has much to offer. Remember to use the filter of God's Word when reading these or any books. They offer helpful information, but not everything they contain agrees with God's Word.

CHAPTER 9:

Epilogue

To some degree, loneliness affects all people of all ages—both male and female, in every imaginable life situation, and whether or not they are Christians. A person doesn't even have to be alone to be lonely! On the other hand, a person doesn't have to be lonely when he or she is alone. Loneliness affects our feelings, thoughts, behaviors, relationships, and spiritual condition. Many different things can trigger it, and it can happen to anyone. The key to the problem is knowing how to deal with it when it hits you.

Loneliness affects our feelings, thoughts, behaviors, relationships, and spiritual condition.

As a Christian, the most important place to start is remembering that you are not alone. You have the assurance from God himself that he is with you at all times. Every day, in every place you go, he is with you to watch over you and care for you. And it is not just that he is there, it is also that he wants you to turn to him with your problems and concerns—feelings of loneliness included. Remember him saying to you "Come to me, all you who are weary and burdened, and I will give you rest. Take my yoke upon you and learn from me, for I am gentle and humble in heart, and you will find rest for your souls" (Matthew 11:28,29). You can turn your worries, anxieties, and blues into prayers to God for help and guidance.

God extends that offer to every member of his family. As a child of God, you are very special to him. To be sure, children of God continue to struggle with the sinful nature. In addition, Satan himself attacks you. He appeals to your sinful nature and uses it against you. When he does, loneliness can be the result. Satan may whisper to you that you are not worth much to anyone, that you are unimportant. But God tells you that, in truth, you *are* important to him. Over and over, God assures you that you are special in his eyes and hold a special place in his family. Here's just one example of your relationship to God.

> For you created my inmost being; you knit me together in my mother's womb. I praise you because I am fearfully and wonderfully made; your works are wonderful, I know that full well. . . . All the days ordained for me were written in your book before one of them came to be. (Psalm 139:13-16)

Each Christian plays a unique role in the kingdom of God. The Scriptures mention on more than one occasion that the kingdom of God, or the church, is the body of Christ. Members of God's family care for one another. When you are feeling lonely, it may seem that nobody cares, but you do have other Christians to whom you can turn for help. You may even find that one day God will put you in a position to help someone else who is experiencing loneliness. Read again what God's Word tells you about the body of Christ.

> God has combined the members of the body . . . so that there should be no division in the body, but that its parts should have equal concern for each other. If one part suffers, every part suffers with it; if one part is honored, every part rejoices with it. Now you are the body of Christ, and each one of you is a part of it. (1 Corinthians 12:24-27)

You can gain much from becoming familiar with your own thoughts, feelings, and behaviors during times of loneliness. In doing so, you can discover where your loneliness comes from. Once you know that, then you can work to conquer your loneliness. You take the first step to conquering your loneliness when you understand what it means to be a child of God. Remember that God was willing to pay a price for you—the precious blood of his one and only Son. The gospel assures you of your value as one of God's children.

> For you know that it was not with perishable things such as silver or gold that you were redeemed . . . but with the precious blood of Christ. (1 Peter 1:18,19)

Stop focusing on the negative circumstances of life and find happiness, joy, and contentment in being the person God has made you. The Lord has given you abilities, inabilities, faith, and a personality. Instead of devaluing yourself, you can begin to view yourself in the light of your heavenly Father's mercy and grace. God made you, redeemed you, and made you his own. What love he has shown you! And it's all simply because HE LOVES YOU! There is no "Yes, but . . ." here. There are no exceptions. It's that simple—he really does love you!

Your understanding of your relationship with God, in view of his mercy, coupled with a healthy self-esteem based on being a child of God in Christ provides your sense of worth.

Chapter 8 provides information about various social skills that can improve your ability to make friends with others. You can do many things to send messages that communicate your desire to meet people and form solid friendships with others. You can do that by what you say, what you do, the way you look. Yet before you can effectively change how you appear to other people, you need the Holy Spirit, through God's message of love, to change how you appear to yourself from within. Your understanding of your relationship with God, in view of his mercy, coupled with a healthy self-esteem based on being a child of God in Christ provides your sense of worth. When you see yourself as being worth something to God in Christ, you can begin to value yourself and reflect that worth to others. What you have to offer to another person in a relationship comes from within yourself. Social skills will only enhance your ability to share that worth with another person. They do not give you that worth. If you allow yourself to slide back into your negative way of thinking, you will continue to doubt that you are worthy of the friendship and love of others.

When you see yourself as being worth something to God in Christ, you can begin to value yourself and reflect that worth to others.

Loneliness? Christians can be lonely?!? Yes, it's true. But it does not have to be permanent. Our prayer is that the Holy Spirit, through the Word, will help put into your mind and soul and heart what you have learned from this book. See yourself and your life in view of God's mercy. You are God's child in Christ, and he is with you always.

> For this God is our God for ever and ever; he will be our guide even to the end. (Psalm 48:14)